OBJECTIVE

proficiency

Erica Hall

Workbook with Answers

WITHDRAWN

CAMBRIDGE
UNIVERSITY PRESS

PUBLISHED BY THE PRESS SYNDICATE OF THE UNIVERSITY OF CAMBRIDGE
The Pitt Building, Trumpington Street, Cambridge, United Kingdom

CAMBRIDGE UNIVERSITY PRESS
The Edinburgh Building, Cambridge CB2 2RU, UK
40 West 20th Street, New York, NY 10011–4211, USA
477 Williamstown Road, Port Melbourne, VIC 3207, Australia
Ruiz de Alarcón 13, 28014 Madrid, Spain
Dock House, The Waterfront, Cape Town 8001, South Africa

http: www.cambridge.org

First published 2002
Third printing 2004

Printed in the United Kingdom at the University Press, Cambridge

Text typeface Minion 11/13.5pt System QuarkXpress® [GECKO]

ISBN 0 521 00030 0 Student's Book
ISBN 0 521 00031 9 Student's Book with Answers
ISBN 0 521 00034 3 Teacher's Book
ISBN 0 521 00032 7 Workbook
ISBN 0 521 00033 5 Workbook with Answers
ISBN 0 521 00035 1 Class Cassette Set

Cover design by Dale Tomlinson

Produced by Gecko Limited, Bicester, Oxon.

Contents

UNIT 1 Ring the changes

Reading

1 You are going to read an article with the headline opposite. Think about the headline and choose the relationship (a–d) which you think the article is most likely to be about.

   a client–supplier   **c** husband–wife
   b boss–employee   **d** parent–child

Quickly read the article to see if you were right.

2 Read the article and decide which paragraph (A–K) each of these cartoons refers to. Underline the sentence(s) or phrase(s) in the text that justify your answer.

SORRY, HONEY, I SHRUNK YOUR JOB PROSPECTS

3 Which of these *do's* and *don'ts* are mentioned in the article? Tick the boxes which apply and circle the sentence(s) or phrase(s) in the text that justify your answer.

a Do not overdo jewellery. ✓
b Attend lots of events. ☐
c Do not over-indulge in food or drink. ☐
d Exercise control when it comes to dancing. ☐
e Be discrete at all times. ☐
f Dress comfortably for all occasions. ☐
g Do not discuss topics of a religious nature. ☐
h Do not break into business discussions. ☐
i Do not refer to your spouse's business expertise. ☐
j Try to have a good time at corporate events. ☐
k Find out something about the host company before the event. ☐
l Give the impression of wanting to know more about the host company. ☐

4 Find a word or phrase in the article with these meanings (the paragraph letter is given in brackets).

a stand in the way of (A)
b skills training (B)
c not particularly wealthy (D)
d price charged (D)
e in the public eye (E)
f increase (F)
g successful achiever (G)
h a useful and valuable resource (I)
i willing to help or please (J)

A Charles Sacarello is talking about an ambitious executive who had almost reached the top of the corporate ladder. There was only one problem that threatened to block his career path – his wife. Bored and lonely sitting at home
5 while her husband was out at work all day, she metamorphosed into a bulldozer at corporate events. She dominated conversations, ploughed her way through trays of canapés and never said 'no' to another glass of champagne.

B Socially inept spouses are Sacarello's bread and butter. The
10 Gibraltar-born image consultant whose firm, Charles & Associates, has become popular in New York, teaches executives' wives – and husbands – how to behave at corporate functions. Spouses hire him for coaching on everything from table manners and how much jewellery to
15 wear ('Don't look like a Christmas tree') to finding the right conversation filler. 'There are bright young men who have made it up the career ladder and their wives don't reflect the position they are trying to occupy,' he says.

C Sacarello's school for executive spouses has proved so
20 popular that he now aims to build up a client base in the UK.

D In New York, Sacarello's clients are upwardly mobile and do a lot of work-related socialising. They are from modest economic backgrounds and range in age from early 20s to late 40s. The fee for an initial consultation is $500; some
25 clients will spend as much as $10,000. They meet Sacarello, 45, and his partner, David Steinberg, 42, in a restaurant. 'We want to see them walk into a room,' Sacarello says. 'Do they skirt off into a corner? Or do they run up and say "hello" because they're nervous?'

30 **E** Some problems – mostly requiring restraint at the buffet table or on the dance floor – are easily solved. Others are more serious. Occasionally, Sacarello has to refer clients to a psychologist or a priest. Many of them are married to high-profile figures from the business and entertainment
35 worlds, so discretion is key. In company files they are referred to by code names.

F 'There are people who have made money but it hasn't bought them polish or class,' Steinberg says. 'We want to boost their self-esteem so they feel comfortable walking into any situation.' Some of his tips are: avoid conversations 40
about sex or religion, do not interrupt if people are talking about business, and never say how wonderful your spouse is in the corporate world.

G Steinberg encourages his clients to enjoy corporate events. 'Know a little bit about the company and show some 45
interest,' he says. 'Our goal is that when two people walk into a room, nobody knows which one is the high-flier.'

H Husbands of high-flying female executives are Sacarello's newest clients. Bill Higgins, 55, a former FBI agent and retired naval captain, found the role of corporate spouse 50
difficult at first. After his retirement in 1997 he started to accompany his wife Barbara Corcoran, 50, who manages Manhattan's largest privately owned real estate company, on business trips. 'I felt uncomfortable because I was the spouse and there were all these guys there who were 55
younger and more successful than me,' he says. Spouses wore different coloured name badges, and Higgins would often be the only man at a table of 40 women, while his wife sat at another table with their husbands.

I Higgins is now so comfortable in his role that he carries a 60
business card labelled 'spouse'. He has formed a men's group to advise other corporate spouses and has set up a website. Corcoran boasts that her husband is an asset at corporate events. 'He comes feeling accomplished and therefore he's willing to dance in my shadow,' she says. 65

J Her first husband was not so obliging: 'He was younger than me and not accomplished. He needed to prove his worth wherever we went. The most awkward moments were when people called him Mr Corcoran.'

K It is the Higgins-Corcoran brand of teamwork that impresses 70
Sacarello. 'One of the main decisions in life is choosing your partner,' he says. 'If you've goofed on that one, how competent are you?'

Vocabulary

5 Hidden in the box are 12 verbs meaning *change* in some way. To find them you need to look horizontally, vertically and diagonally in the direction of the arrows. The first one is done for you. When you have found them, choose the most appropriate one to complete each sentence below. You may need to change the form of the verb. Use your dictionary to help you.

A	C	E	F	I	G	U	R	T	R	A	N	S	D
C	O	N	V	E	R	T	R	E	T	C	O	E	X
B	R	E	T	L	A	L	T	A	R	R	V	V	Y
F	A	T	T	A	U	L	D	R	E	E	M	O	P
G	O	A	N	D	D	N	I	L	L	V	E	L	S
B	A	U	N	M	E	A	P	O	R	I	S	V	M
M	E	T	A	M	O	R	P	H	O	S	E	E	U
E	X	C	A	U	N	D	O	T	R	E	L	S	T
P	R	U	N	N	I	N	I	B	L	L	Y	G	A
G	A	L	L	U	M	R	O	F	S	N	A	R	T
Z	I	F	H	E	R	F	U	J	Y	W	A	S	E

→ ← ↓ ↑ ↙ ↘ ↗

a The good thing about children is that they .... very easily to new environments.
b I took the coat back to the shop to have it ....
c In line 20, 'men' should be .... to 'people'.
d The design proposals were unpopular and only accepted in a .... form.
e These bacteria have .... into forms that are resistant to certain drugs.
f The reorganisation will totally .... the British entertainment industry.
g The awkward boy I knew had .... into a tall, handsome man.
h They live in a .... windmill.
i How do we know that humans .... from apes?
j Vegetable prices .... according to the season.
k The bank manager forced them to .... their sales forecasts three times.
l What started out as a short story eventually .... into a full-scale novel.

6 Complete these sentences, which all include expressions with *change*, using the picture clues below and your dictionary to help you. Which of the sentences have no corresponding illustration?

EXAMPLE: She's always been against the supermarket, but she soon changed her ..tune.. when she realised what they would pay for her land.

a She'd been with the same company such a long time, she felt she needed a change of ....
b That Italian restaurant is nowhere near as good since it changed ....
c Could you change the .... for me?
d If he wants to carry on living here, he's going to have to change his ....
e When I first met him, I didn't like him, but now I've changed my ....
f I've changed the .... in the guest room.
g I wouldn't change .... with him for the world!
h She took a change of .... in her suitcase as they were staying overnight.
i Let's change the .... or we'll end up arguing again.

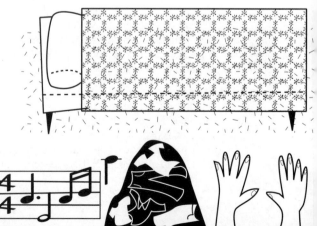

7 Using these verbs and prepositions, make an appropriate two- or three-part phrasal verb to replace each verb in italics in the sentences below. You may need to change the form of the verb and the word order. Use your dictionary to help you.

	across	
	around	
	down (× 2)	
carry (× 2)	in	
get (× 6)	into	for
make (× 2)	off (× 2)	with (× 2)
turn (× 4)	on (× 2)	
	out (× 2)	
	over	
	up	

EXAMPLE: He paused for a moment to listen and then *continued* eating.
He paused for a moment to listen and then **carried on** eating.

a She came out of the shop to find thieves had *stolen* her bicycle.
b The chaos in the house was starting to *depress* him.
c Most wild animals won't *attack* humans unless they are provoked.
d Boy, will I be glad to *finish* these exams!
e It *transpired* that Mr Keller and I had both been to the same school.
f He has to *submit* the application form by Friday.
g News of someone's pregnancy soon *spreads*.
h You'll find my enthusiasm more than *offsets* my lack of experience.
i How successful were they in *conveying* the message, do you think?
j The hospital is *conducting* tests to find out what is wrong with her.
k Could you *despatch* the parcel this morning, please?
l No sooner had the witch cast her spell than the prince *became* a frog.
m Her request for time off work was *denied*.

Grammar

8 Complete these extracts with an appropriate form of the verbs in brackets.

I (1) .... (find) myself in some bizarre situations recently, but none so unusual as this: lying on a black plastic mattress, covered from head to toe in oil, with a man walking all over me.
Incense (2) .... (burn) on a low table, the only sounds that of the sea and of crows ducking out of the way of an eagle. If I (3) .... (be) in Africa or the Caribbean this might (4) .... (be) part of some full-moon voodoo ritual, and I would (5) .... (be) concerned about my safety. But this (6) .... (be) the middle of another hot and slightly steamy day in southern India, and whatever (7) .... (happen) to me (8) .... (be done) in the name of health. I (9) .... (experience) my first Ayurveda rejuvenation massage.

As those first months (10) .... (pass) and we all (11) .... (settle) into our new existence together, I (12) .... (realise) just what friends (13) .... (mean) when they (14) .... (try) to explain to me the joy of having one's own child. No matter how eloquently it (15) .... (be described), nobody (16) .... (be) able to get anywhere near the real experience. We (17) .... (look) back on all our previous worries about how our lives would be changed and disrupted, and (18) .... (be) shocked by how irrelevant those thoughts now (19) .... (seem). It was as if we (20) .... (just be handed) the key to crack the next part of the code of existence. The various loves in me (21) .... (grow) and (22) .... (grow), and all as a result of this new being who (23) .... (come) to stay in our home. And to think that we might (24) .... (go) through life without ever having let this happen to us.

UNIT 2 Expectations

Summary skills

1 Quickly read through the text below and choose the best heading (**a–d**).

    a The truth about camels
    b Travel by camel
    c Living with a camel
    d Why camels should be avoided

IN THIS MECHANISED AND INDUSTRIAL EPOCH, the camel does not seem to be an obvious choice of travelling companion when sophisticated cross-country vehicles exist for the toughest of terrains. Add to this the stockpile of derisory and mocking myths, truths and sayings about the camel and one is forced to ask the question: why use camels at all?

Purely as a means of getting from A to B when time is the most important factor, the camel should not even be considered. As a means of transport for scientific groups who wish to carry out useful research in the field, the camel is limiting. It can be awkward and risky transporting delicate equipment and specimens. However, for the individual, small group and expedition wishing to see the desert as it should be seen, the camel is an unrivalled means of transport.

From my own personal point of view, the primary reason must be that, unlike any motorised vehicle, camels allow you to integrate completely with the desert and the people within it – something it is impossible to do at 80 kph enclosed in a 'tin can'. A vehicle in the desert can be like a prison cell and the constant noise of the engine tends to blur all sense of the solitude, vastness and deafening quiet which are so intrinsic to the experience.

2 Read the first paragraph again and choose the best summary sentence (**a–c**).

    a Not only are camels unable to compete with modern, all-terrain 4 x 4 vehicles, they are neither easy nor pleasant to travel with.
    b The existence of advanced, all-terrain four-wheel drives and the wealth of anecdotal evidence against the camel make it unsuitable as a means of transport in this day and age.
    c In this day and age of advanced, all-powerful off-road vehicles, camels are perhaps not the most logical transport option, even without the bad press they have received over the years.

3 Read the rest of the text again and tick the points which are included. The first one is done for you.

    a becoming one with the environment ✓
    b conducting scientific fieldwork ☐
    c providing safe, secure transport in remote regions ☐
    d experiencing the emptiness, space and silence of the desert ☐
    e covering distances quickly ☐
    f gaining access to the desert proper ☐
    g conveying fragile cargoes ☐
    h requiring minimal equipment/stores ☐

4 Complete these summary sentences using the points in exercise 3 to help you.

    a Camels cannot be recommended for

    .... ,
    for .... or
    for ....

    b Camels are second to none, however, for

    .... ,
    for .... and
    for ....

Grammar

5   Complete these extracts with an appropriate form of the verbs in the boxes. You may also need to use *will/shall* alone and in some passages you may need to include another modal verb in your answer. There may be more than one correct answer.

be (× 6)	be on the brink of	celebrate	check	get
give	head	help	leave	like
manage	open	pack	show	visit

acquire	also consider	be (× 2)
develop	also expect	

To... Emma-Jane Davis
From ... Lizzie Clark
Subject: Another time...?

Thanks for the invite for this evening – I (1) .... able to make it though. Hugh (2) .... for Mexico in the morning (his plane (3) .... at 5.00 a.m.!) and he (4) .... hard-pushed to get ready in time. It looks like I (5) .... him into the small hours. His company (6) .... an office there next month and apparently some problem's come up with the lease they (7) .... signing. If he (8) .... to sort everything out, he (9) .... over the moon and I guess the company (10) .... too! Anyhow, sorry about this evening but (11) .... we do something together at the weekend? I (12) .... my grandmother at some point during the day on Sunday, but otherwise I (13) .... free till Hugh (14) .... back at the end of next week. Unfortunately Susan (15) .... around, she (16) .... her birthday at the beach (did you know she (17) .... 37 on Saturday??), but I (18) .... what films (19) .... in the evening if you (20) .... That (21) .... me something to look forward to when I (22) .... suitcases tonight! Let me know how you're fixed.

Earth Observation Applications Scientist

Leading a specialist team, you (23) .... a generic synthetic aperture radar (SAR) image focusing processor, with the aim of producing a cost-effective high performance space radar within two years. Ideally you (24) .... a minimum of five years' experience in signal processing applications plus signal simulation experience, though candidates with less experience but a highly relevant academic background (25) .... Excellent computing skills (26) .... necessary and you (27) .... to have a good understanding of advanced engineering mathematics. Proven analytical and presentation skills (28) .... essential to your success, as (29) .... your effective use of IT systems.

---

be likely to	break	have	move	remain (× 2)

5-Day Forecast

After a fine and mainly dry start to the week, rain (30) .... in to the north-west of Scotland later. England and Wales (31) .... stay fairly settled with further spells of sunshine for the second half of the week, although western parts (32) .... some patchy rain on Thursday. Scotland (33) .... cloudy and damp with rain and drizzle, especially over the mountains on Tuesday, before brighter weather (34) .... through on Wednesday, particularly in the west. The rest of the week (35) .... changeable with a lot of cloud and some light rain but also a few spells of sunshine.

Vocabulary

6 Complete these sentences using a verb from the box. Change the form of the verb if necessary and use your dictionary to help you.

arm	elbow	eye	face	head
mouth	rib	shoulder	thumb	voice

a She .... the other passengers suspiciously.
b It looks to me as if the singers are only .... the words.
c They .... the onlookers aside.
d Teachers cannot be expected to .... all the blame for poor exam results.
e Nobody knows who is .... the terrorists.
f He has .... his nose at authority all his life.
g His brothers .... him about his new girlfriend.
h She .... one of Britain's leading travel firms.
i We have to .... the facts and start cutting costs.
j Leading educationalists have .... their concern over the new proposals.

7 Using an appropriate word from the box with *have no*, replace the words in italics so that each sentence has the *opposite* meaning. You will also need to change the form of some verbs and may need to add a preposition or *but*. Use your dictionary to help you.

appeal	chance	desire	doubt
option	problem	qualms	recollection

EXAMPLE: Apparently, he *remembered* our meeting last March.
Apparently, he **had no recollection of** our meeting last March.

a Having known him for years, she *didn't believe* that he was guilty.
b They *found it difficult* to follow the instructions that they had been given.
c Eng *really wanted* to go back to her home country before she died.
d Sara *was unhappy* about lying to the police.
e I *will be able to* finish this essay before the weekend.
f Having run out of money, Bogdan *chose* to work.
g Going to the theatre *was a treat* after everything she had been through.

Use of English

8 Read the text below and use the words given in capitals at the end of some of the lines to form a word that fits in the space in the same line. There is an example at the beginning (0).

More people fly today than ever before, yet many – experienced air (0) *travellers*   TRAVEL
as well as novices – suffer anguish and (1) .... at the mere thought   APPREHEND
of flying. As many as one out of seven people are thought to experience anxiety
when flying, with women (2) .... men two to one in these feelings of   NUMBER
(3) ....   QUIET
    A certain amount of concern is (4) .... The sheer size of modern   STAND
jet aircraft, which appear awkward and (5) .... on the ground, makes   WIELD
one wonder how they will manage to get into the air – and stay there. Most of these
fears are (6) .... and are perhaps based on the knowledge that once in   LOGIC
the aircraft, we, as passengers, are (7) .... to control our fate, which   POWER
depends solely on the (8) .... of the crew. There is little comfort for us   EXPERT
in the numerous statistical compilations which show that modern air transport is
many times safer than transport by car or rail.
    Most people's fear remains on a (9) .... scale. For others, however,   MANAGE
the anxiety can become an overwhelming fear, known as *aviophobia*. Symptoms
include feelings of panic, sweating, palpitations, depression, (10) .... ,   SLEEP
weeping spells and sometimes temporary paralysis.

9 For questions 1–15, read the text below and think of the word which best fits each space. Use only one word in each space. There is an example at the beginning (0).

Rural idylls tempt the adventurous

A new word has entered (0) ......*the*...... lexicon of travel brochures, (1) .... which has also been cropping (2) .... on rural road signs far (3) .... Europe's crowded beaches.

'Agritourism' is a new holiday flavour, sought by growing numbers of holidaymakers (4) .... want to taste a little of the real country, to breathe its air, savour its food and wine, perhaps to speak its language.

The pioneer project (5) .... agritourism was the development of gîtes in France. Government grants in the postwar years helped convert crumbling farm outbuildings (6) .... rural holiday cottages for poor Parisians, (7) .... the British became beneficiaries in the early 1970s.

(8) .... 17 years from 1978, the number of Britons taking a gîte holiday increased (9) .... year. (10) .... agritourism has become a philosophy (11) .... embraces properties across the Mediterranean, with Cyprus, Spain and Italy (12) .... the forefront of development.

Agritourism might manifest (13) .... as en-suite guest rooms on a working farm, rustic quarters in a restored country cottage or a grand, antique-filled mansion with its (14) .... pool. It may be a revitalised winery, a cheese-making dairy or a village co-operative reviving traditional handicrafts. But it (15) .... certainly be rural – and often remote.

Reading

1 You are going to read four extracts which are all concerned in some way with unusual behaviour. For questions 1–8, choose the answer (A, B, C or D) which you think fits best according to the text.

Blanca stayed behind in the country with her parents for a few more days. It was then that Clara began having nightmares, walking in her sleep, and waking up screaming. During the day, she went about half in a dream, seeing premonitions in the animals' behavior: the hens were not laying their daily eggs, the cows were acting frightened, the dogs were howling to death, the rats, spiders, and worms were coming out of their hiding places, the birds were leaving their nests and flying off in great formations, while her pigeons were screaming with hunger in the treetops. She stared obsessively at the frail column of white smoke that was issuing from the volcano, and peered at the changes in the color of the sky. Blanca made her all sorts of soothing teas and warm baths, and Esteban resorted to the old box of homeopathic pills to calm her down, but her nightmares continued.

'There's going to be an earthquake!' Clara announced, daily growing paler and more agitated.

'For God's sake, Clara, there are always quakes!' Esteban replied.

'This time it's going to be different. There will be ten thousand dead.'

'There aren't even that many people in the whole country,' he said, laughing.

1 Clara was having nightmares because she was disturbed by
  A Blanca's continued presence in the country.
  B her inability to sleep at night.
  C her anticipation of what was going to happen.
  D the announcement of an impending earthquake.

2 Which of these best describes Esteban's response to Clara?
  A He was dismissive.
  B He was worried.
  C He was furious.
  D He was amused.

The monarch of the glen* isn't all he's cracked up to be. Male red deer are scared of bad weather, according to British researchers, and when a storm brews the stags are more likely to move to sheltered grazing areas than the tougher females.

Larissa Conradt of the University of Leeds and her colleagues at the University of Cambridge investigated the grazing behaviour of red deer on the Scottish island of Rhum in winter and spring, when food is short.

When the weather is calm, both sexes prefer to graze the high-quality open grassland on the island. But when bad weather sets in, the researchers found that males are the first to depart these areas for more sheltered sites, despite poorer grazing there. This is the first evidence that the weather contributes to habitat segregation of male and female deer, as well as other hoofed mammals—an idea dubbed the 'weather sensitivity hypothesis'.

This is counter-intuitive, says Conradt. You would expect males to be less sensitive to the weather, because their larger size should allow them to retain heat better. But a theoretical model devised by the researchers suggests this isn't so. Although they have bigger mouths than the females, the stags can't eat enough to warm their excessive bulk and offset the chilling effects of the weather. Sheltering during stormy conditions is the only way that males can stop themselves losing too much heat.

*The Monarch of the Glen is the title of a famous painting of a magnificent male deer (stag) by Sir Edwin Landseer (1802–73)

Bright Light – the light that leaves you beaming

BANISH THE WINTER BLUES FOR JUST £129.99

'Winter Blues' for many of us can mean listlessness, irritability, increased appetite and even depression – and it's largely due to lack of sunlight. 'Bright Light' therapy has long been used all over Northern Europe to help alleviate these symptoms; improving and regulating low energy levels, mood and sleep patterns. As little as an hour a day can be all that's needed to lift the spirits of those who simply feel under the weather at this time of year. Today's offer is for the Innosol 236 Bright Light from Finland, where the winter sun is scarce and bright lights were developed. Some 10 times brighter than ordinary house lights, you can enjoy your 'light bath' whilst having breakfast or reading a book – there's no need to look directly into the light although it is quite safe to do so. Measuring 50cm H × 21cm W × 8cm D, the Innosol 236 is mains powered and comes with 2.1m cord and fitted, earthed plug. Weighing around 2kgs, the unit is fully portable and features a built-in stand. It may also be wall-mounted if required. On offer for just £129.99 including postage and packing, saving £40.00 off the recommended retail price.

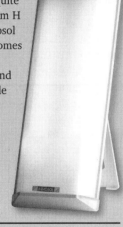

Order yours today!

3 Male red deer move to sheltered areas before females in bad weather because
A males are more frightened of storms than females.
B males are not as tough as females.
C males prefer to withdraw from females in bad weather.
D males feel the cold more than females.

4 What discovery did Larissa Conradt find most surprising?
A The bigger the animal, the bigger the mouth.
B The bigger the animal, the less it can eat.
C The bigger the animal, the more shelter it needs.
D The bigger the animal, the more food it needs.

5 What claim is made of 'Bright Light' therapy?
A It prevents the onset of lethargy and low spirits in winter.
B It counteracts the effects of sunlight deprivation.
C It has a history of extensive use throughout Europe.
D It requires less than seven hours a week to be effective.

6 What does the advertisement say about the Innosol 236?
A It's made by a well-known company.
B It's cheap to run.
C It's medically approved.
D It's versatile and convenient.

The end seemed very near for Hudson, a Canadian Eskimo dog tethered near the shore of Hudson Bay east of Churchill, Manitoba. A thousand-pound polar bear was lumbering toward the dog and about 40 others, the prized possessions of Brian Ladoon, a hunter and trapper. It was mid-November; ice had not yet formed on the bay, and the open water prevented bears from hunting their favourite prey, seals. So this bear had been virtually fasting for four months. Surely a dog was destined to become a meal.

The bear closed in. Did Hudson howl in terror and try to flee? On the contrary. He wagged his tail, grinned, and actually bowed to the bear, as if in invitation. The bear responded with enthusiastic body language and nonaggressive facial signals. These two normally antagonistic species were speaking the same language: 'Let's play!'

The romp was on. For several minutes dog and bear wrestled and cavorted. Once the bear completely wrapped himself around the dog like a friendly white cloud. Bear and dog then embraced, as if in sheer abandon.

Every evening for more than a week the bear returned to play with one of the dogs. Finally the ice formed, and he set off for his winter habitat.

This behaviour has been witnessed repeatedly in Churchill but has not been reported elsewhere in the Arctic. Throughout the region, polar bears occasionally kill and eat sled dogs.

7 Why didn't Hudson try to run away when the bear approached?
   A He was tied up.
   B He was ready to play.
   C He was unfamiliar with bears.
   D He was an unusual dog.

8 Why did the bear leave?
   A He could now reach his feeding ground.
   B The weather changed for the worse.
   C He never stayed anywhere too long.
   D He got fed up of playing with the dogs.

Grammar

2 Identify the incorrect verb form in these sentences, then rewrite each sentence correctly starting with the word in brackets.

EXAMPLE: Clara would not have been ill, if she didn't suspect the imminent earthquake.
(Had …)
didn't suspect → hadn't suspected

Had Clara **not suspected** the imminent earthquake, she would not have been ill.

a If male deer wouldn't shelter in bad weather, it could be a matter of life and death for them.
(Unless …)

b Unless Bright Light therapy has become more widely available, the number of winter blues sufferers won't fall.
(Provided …)

c If you would happen to notice anything strange, kindly make a note of it for me.
(Should …)

d Were jetlag a figment of the imagination, air travellers had no problems on arrival at their destination.
(If …)

e As the sun should cause permanent damage to your eyes, you shouldn't look directly at it.
(Given that …)

f This planet would be heading for destruction, unless we pay more attention to environmental issues.
(If …)

g Provided you stay calm, we would be able to assess the situation quickly.
(If …)

h If we hadn't had luck on our side, we hadn't ever survived the storm and returned safe and sound.
(Without …)

i If there is a red sky at night, it is fine the next day.
(As long as …)

j If you spend long periods of time above 5500 metres, you must experience the ill effects of altitude.
(Provided …)

k You would have no evidence to support your theory now, if you didn't persevere with your research.
(But for …)

l Unless you took time to acclimatise when you arrive in a hot country, you will be asking for trouble.
(As long as …)

m I'll agree to come to the party as long as you haven't worn those ridiculous trousers.
(On condition that …)

Vocabulary

3

The words in capitals in these sentences are all anagrams of nouns meaning *behaviour*. Use the context and your dictionary to help you solve them.

EXAMPLE: It's considered good RENMANS in some societies to leave a little food on your plate. *manners*

a Over the years we've got used to his funny little YAWS.

b His NOCTIAS since that morning have been quite eccentric and unpredictable.

c The president surprised everyone with his unusual TUNCCOD at the memorial service.

d She walked at the head of the procession, her GIRABEN proud and distinguished.

e The actors were given lessons in speech and TREMENDOPT.

f There was nothing in his REUMANDEO that suggested he was anxious.

g His eating STIHBA are rather extraordinary.

4

Correct any words in these sentences which are used or spelled incorrectly.

a The Santa Ana wind can have a dramatic affect on people in Los Angeles.

b In some extreme weather conditions, people have been known to loose control.

c Certain weather patterns are associated with a raise in crime rates.

d Predicting the weather accurately takes more than practise.

e My grandfather believes in weather lore like his descendants before him.

f The day the weather forecasters took industrious action was an interesting day for the nation.

g Some people believe animal behaviour could offer a viable alternate means of earthquake detection.

h Beside being struck twice by lightning, she has also had some experiences of hurricanes.

5

Match each adjective on the left with the most appropriate noun on the right to make collocations that complete the sentences below. Use your dictionary to help you. There may be more than one correct answer.

bad	feeling
female	foreboding
funny	hunch
second	intuition
serious	misgivings
sixth	omen
sneaking	sense
strange	sight
strong	sign
sure	suspicion

EXAMPLE: Many teachers have expressed .....*serious*..... .....*misgivings*..... about the new exams.

a Those black clouds are a .... of rain.

b The detective had a .... that he was onto something.

c He had a .... that something terrible was about to happen.

d I once met a man with .... who told me I was going to lose my job – and I did.

e I had a .... that you'd show up!

f I've got a .... that we're going the wrong way.

g We hoped that the delay at the airport was not a .... for our holiday.

h .... told him that they would be waiting for him when he got home.

i When a woman anticipates something, it is sometimes put down to ....

PRIVATE EYE

gone to hunch

UNIT 4 Sweet rituals

Summary skills

1 Quickly read through the text below about the Greek cheese, feta. Where do you think it comes from?

    a a guidebook on Greece
    b a daily newspaper
    c a food magazine
    d a book on European farming

Greeks consume more cheese per person than any other Europeans (slightly more than the French), and the majority of
5 it is the most well known of all Greek cheeses, feta. Feta, in some form, is rarely missing from a Greek table as it complements all kinds of food.
10 Feta is made mainly from sheep's milk, often with a small amount of goat's milk. Traditional sheep's milk feta is very white. Good feta should be moist, with a
15 fresh, slightly sour and pleasantly salty taste, but not all feta has the same flavour. There are two main categories: cheese that matures in wooden barrels, and cheese
20 that matures in tins. Within these categories there are over 10 regional varieties. Barrel-matured feta is generally considered to be the more tasty as the cheese
25 gains a woody flavour.

The production of feta is simple in theory, but needs extremely skilled cheese-makers to ensure it has the right taste and texture.
30 The cheese curds are salted twice: half an hour after they are placed in the moulds, and again an hour later. This procedure means the cheese remains fresh for about
35 a year or even longer, since the salt prevents the development of the micro-organisms that would have

made it a completely different, much harder and sharper cheese.
40 About four kilos of milk are needed to produce one kilo of feta and the cheese is ready to eat two months later.

'The secret of feta is in the
45 salting,' says Stathis Karayanni. The two of us are drinking ouzo at a taverna in Davlia, near his cheese factory just below Mount Parnassus. 'At a precise moment,
50 you cut a piece from the centre of the barrel,' he says. 'It should taste pleasantly salted and fresh – not too salty, but not too sweet either because, without the right
55 amount of salt, the cheese will spoil. At that stage you can still correct it – wash off some salt, or add a little as needed. But you have to act when the time is
60 right, otherwise it's too late.'

The various regional plants that the sheep graze on determine the taste of the milk they will produce. Stathis tells me he tries to buy
65 milk only from farmers whose sheep graze in the higher parts of Mount Parnassus, where the wild greens are far more diverse and aromatic. 'Sheep that are fed only
70 commercial food produce tasteless milk, which makes bland feta,' he says. Seasonal plants, as well as slight variations in manufacture, play an important
75 role in the taste of feta. My own favourite is from Parnassus. It has a smooth and creamy texture, and is best when very fresh and soft, preferably no more than three or
80 four months old.

2 Read the text and complete the table.

Attributes of good feta

Factors influencing the flavour of feta

3 Compare this paragraph with the information in the text on how feta is produced. Delete any sentences which are not based on the text. In the sentences which are left, underline any phrases which are taken directly from the text.

Although simple in theory, the production of feta needs extremely skilled cheese-makers. Once the milk has been delivered, it is left to curdle, then 'cut'. The curds are put into moulds and set aside to drain. The secret of feta is in the salting of the curds, which happens twice – half an hour after they are placed in the moulds and again an hour later. This procedure prevents the development of the micro-organisms that would have made a much sharper tasting cheese. The feta is then left to mature in either tins or wooden barrels.

4 Write your own paragraph summarising how feta is produced according to the text, using words and phrases from the box to replace the ones you have underlined in exercise 3. Try to keep your summary to 70 words or less.

bacteria	great skill	growth
have been poured into	in principle	lies in the way
key to good feta	not difficult	process
manufacture of feta	prohibits	requires
which would make	salt is added to	
30 minutes and 90 minutes		

Use of English

5 For questions 1–6, think of one word only which can be used appropriately in all three sentences.

1 I hate travelling by ......*air*...... because I usually get horribly sick.

Venice in winter has always appealed for its ......*air*...... of mystery and sadness.

Sadly, the ......*air*...... in my home town has become increasingly polluted.

2 His parents were so relieved when he finally got a .... job.

In ......*decent*...... rain, the crowd waited patiently for a bus to take them home.

Although she was nervous, her voice was .... as she welcomed everyone to the recital.

3 Even as a child he loved ......*nature*...... and enjoyed being in the countryside.

The severity of the punishment depends very much on the ......*nature*...... of the crime.

She has a lovely sunny ......*nature*...... – everyone loves her and always has.

4 It was the second time she had fallen .... and badly bruised her shoulder.

To do the job effectively, it helps if you are quite .... built.

According to intelligence reports, the terrorists are .... armed.

5 He went to the library to ......*get*...... two books on oriental cookery.

They were planning to ......*return*...... home by midnight but they were running late.

With lives at stake, the police had no alternative but to ......*open*...... fire.

6 She claims her article was a ......*fair*...... comment on a matter of public interest.

Once again ......*fair*...... weather was forecast for the following day.

Like her mother, she is tall and pretty, with ......*dark*...... hair and blue eyes.

Grammar

6   Complete this extract from a book by Indian cookery writer Madhur Jaffrey, using an appropriate form of the verbs in brackets. Be careful to use a passive, *would / used to* or a modal where necessary. There may be more than one correct answer.

I (0) ..*have always loved*.... (always love) to eat well. My mother once (1) .... (inform) me that my passion (2) .... (date back) to the hour of my birth when my grandmother (3) .... (write) the sacred syllable 'Om' ('I am') on my tongue with a finger dipped in fresh honey. I (4) .... (apparently observe) smacking my lips rather loudly. Starting from that time, food – good food – (5) .... (just appear) miraculously from somewhere at the back of our house in Delhi. It (6) .... (precede) by the most tantalising odours and the sounds of crockery and cutlery on the move. Soon we (7) .... (all sit) around the dinner table, engrossed in eating monsoon mushrooms cooked with coriander and turmeric, fish that my brothers (8) .... (just catch) in the Jamuna River and cubes of lamb smothered in a yoghurt sauce.

Indian food (9) .... (be) far more varied than the menus of Indian restaurants (10) .... (suggest). One of my fondest memories of school in Delhi (11) .... (be) of the lunches that we (12) .... (all bring) from our homes, ensconced in multi-tiered lunchboxes. My stainless steel lunchbox (13) .... (dangle) from the handle of my bicycle as I (14) .... (ride) at great speed to school every morning, my ribboned pigtails fluttering behind me. When the lunch bell finally (15) .... (set) us free, my friends and I (16) .... (assemble) under a shady tree if it (17) .... (be) summer or on a sunny verandah if it (18) .... (be) winter. My mouth (19) .... (begin) to water even before we (20) .... (open up) our lunchboxes. Eating (21) .... (always fill) us with a sense of adventure and discovery as we (22) .... (can) not always anticipate what the others (23) .... (bring).

Vocabulary

7   Which of these adjectives describe flavour and which describe texture? Write F (flavour) or T (texture). Use your dictionary to help you. The first one is done for you.

aromatic	[F]	bland	[ ]
clotted	[ ]	creamy	[ ]
delectable	[ ]	grainy	[ ]
hard	[ ]	insipid	[ ]
light	[ ]	moist	[ ]
mushy	[ ]	palatable	[ ]
salty	[ ]	savoury	[ ]
set	[ ]	smooth	[ ]
tasteless	[ ]	tasty	[ ]
unappetising	[ ]	woody	[ ]

8   Complete these compound adjectives with a word that fits. There may be more than one correct answer. Use your dictionary to help you.

EXAMPLE: ice-..*cold*.. water

a   a thirst-................. drink
b   a mouth-................. smell
c   a fast-................. outlet
d   free-................. eggs
e   all-................. biscuits
f   low-................. yoghurt
g   fresh-................. bread

h   Japanese-................. cooking
i   stir-................. vegetables
j   wafer-................. slices
k   sun-................. tomatoes
l   soft-................. chocolates
m   full-................. wine
n   home-................. food

9 Complete this text with words from the box.

chef	cultures
different	fresh
masters	natural
poach	quality
sharpening	vegetables

The Japanese are (**1**) .... of fish and its preparation. Compare our two (**2**) .... on this subject. We would take a superb (**3**) .... piece of fish, (**4**) ...., sauce and serve it with potatoes and (**5**) .... Quite delicious it would be, too.

Give the same piece of fish to a Japanese (**6**) .... and he would probably serve the prepared flesh in its uncooked state with a little soy and Japanese horseradish. This would also be delicious, but in an entirely (**7**) .... way. The salt (**8**) .... of the soy would emphasise the (**9**) .... flavour of the uncooked fish, with the horseradish adding a final (**10**) .... to the flavour.

Use of English

10 Complete the second sentence so that it has a similar meaning to the first sentence using the word given. Do not change the word given. You must use between three and eight words, including the word given.

EXAMPLE:

0 The family moved to the capital ten years ago.

home

The capital .... ten years now.

The gap can be filled by the words 'has been home to the family for'.

1 The Portuguese probably introduced chilli peppers to Asia.

thought

Chilli peppers ....
to Asia by the Portuguese.

2 People think he succeeded through hard work and determination.

put

People ....
hard work and determination.

3 Greeks consume more cheese per capita than any other Europeans.

consumption

Greece ....
in Europe.

4 Everyone must have noticed the change in temperature.

failed

No one ....
the change in temperature.

5 He even divulged the secret of good feta.

far

He ....
the secret of good feta.

6 Apparently, he applied to take leave but his boss said no.

down

Apparently, his ....
by his boss.

7 If you have no experience, getting a job can be impossible.

unless

It can be impossible ....
experience.

8 The organisers went out of their way to help.

not

The organisers .... helpful.

Reading

1   For questions 1–18, read the three texts below and decide
    which answer (A, B, C or D) best fits each gap.

The world's your high street

Sure you can buy virtually anything from anywhere over the
Internet. But there's still nothing quite like the real retail
therapy experience. So why not (1) .... yourself and take a
trip to New York, the consumer (2) .... of the world. Home
to Macy's, Tiffany's, Saks 5th Avenue, Bloomingdales and
countless other (3) .... names, 'the Big Apple' (4) ....
some of the most famous and glamorous stores you'll find
anywhere on Earth. A stroll around this vibrant city is
shopping heaven.

Then, after a hard day's shopping you're spoilt for choice for
places to (5) .... your feet up. Relax at the (6) .... Blue
Note jazz club in Greenwich Village, or choose from the city's
thousands of bars, clubs, diners and restaurants, each with
its own unique atmosphere.
New York offers even the most jaded traveller a sensory
experience that's unforgettable. And for shopping, as any
New Yorker will proudly tell you, there ain't no place like it!

1 A value	B comfort	C treat	D flatter
2 A society	B capital	C paradise	D community
3 A department	B consumer	C shopping	D household
4 A sites	B flaunts	C boasts	D benefits
5 A lay	B rest	C place	D put
6 A dissimilar	B incomparable	C inestimable	D unmeasurable

Worst-off shoppers in Europe

British consumers have up to 40% less spending
power than those in America and Europe, according
to a new (7) ....
Even though income taxes and social security
contributions are far higher on the Continent, workers
are paid more and (8) .... less for most goods and
services. As a result, the average British shopper has 40%
less disposable income than his German neighbour.
The figure emerges in a survey which (9) .... the average
income, before and after tax, throughout western Europe
and in America, together with the average (10) .... of
living, to work out the difference in spending power
between nations.
According to the survey, (11) .... by the William M
Mercer consultancy, Britons are 37% poorer than the
Dutch, 22% worse off than the French and 15% poorer
than the Americans.
The 'spending power squeeze' is so acute that more than
a third of Britons cannot afford a holiday and 26% are
living below the (12) .... line.

7 A study	B record	C research	D source
8 A liable	B charged	C available	D costed
9 A compared	B contrasted	C matched	D corresponded
10 A price	B value	C cost	D index
11 A sorted through	B sorted out	C carried through	D carried out
12 A poverty	B family	C official	D party

Brainstorming turns our heads

When Isaac Newton was asked how he discovered the (13) .... of gravity, he answered: 'I thought about it all the time.' It was as simple as that.

If Newton were asked the same question today, he would be more (14) .... to say: 'Well, there was a bunch of us round a table. We were meant to be (15) .... with ideas for a new apple sauce. And so we had to imagine we were an apple, hanging on a tree. How did we feel? And then Sally from Human Resources said, 'I feel heavy, so heavy'. And then I thought ...'

He would, in other (16) .... , have been in a brainstorming session. Born on Madison Avenue in the 1950s, brainstorming was long considered the preserve of those wild and crazy folk in advertising. In more recent years, however, it has (17) .... into the mainstream and is now used by business of all kinds, not to (18) .... everyone from civil servants to scientists and engineers or, indeed, anyone with a problem to solve.

13	**A** law	**B** order	**C** doctrine	**D** formula
14	**A** inclined	**B** probable	**C** prone	**D** likely
15	**A** thinking up	**B** coming up	**C** coming out	**D** thinking out
16	**A** words	**B** terms	**C** hands	**D** circumstances
17	**A** diffused	**B** extended	**C** diversified	**D** spread
18	**A** neglect	**B** omit	**C** mention	**D** forget

Grammar

2 Which of these nouns are countable, which are uncountable and which can be either? Use your dictionary to help you complete the table. The first one has been done for you.

Noun	Countable	Uncountable	Noun	Countable	Uncountable
advice	✗	✓	machinery		
appliance			money		
business			parking		
cash			preference		
clothing			produce		
competition			product		
complaint			promotion		
equipment			publicity		
experience			right		
furniture			shopping		
information			success		

3 Use words from exercise 2 to complete these sentences. Sometimes you will need to use the words on their own, sometimes you will need to add *a/an, the, some* or *any*. There may be more than one correct answer.

a You've bought a lovely house and it will look great once you get .... in.

b When my grandmother was a child, ... such as washing machines and dishwashers did not exist.

c We have received .... from a dissatisfied customer in Sweden.

d A huge percentage of new products coming to the market will fail; .... are harder to achieve.

e I've been asked to take part in .... which the company's doing on its new skin care range.

f Apparently .... at the new store is free to motorists who spend over a certain sum there.

g If there is a choice of colours, do you have .... ?

h Is there a bank around here where I can change .... ?

i .... generated by the court case is hardly what the manufacturers would have wanted.

j When credit and debit cards are so widely accepted these days, I don't see the point in carrying ....

k Although he enjoys his work, he tries hard not to let .... interfere with pleasure.

l .... in the retail sector are likely to see their profits hit.

m By entering .... every week, she reckons on winning something at least four times a year!

n .... from other countries has seen many companies go out of business.

4 Which of the verb forms in italics in these sentences are correct? Sometimes the singular verb is correct, sometimes the plural verb is correct and sometimes both are correct. Delete the options which *don't* apply.

EXAMPLE: Athletics *is/~~are~~* on TV this afternoon.

a Belongings *is/are* sometimes a burden.
b Your clothes *is/are* very smart.
c The committee *votes/vote* on the issue tonight.
d The economy *is/are* in a state of decline.
e A new family *has/have* moved in next door.
f The goods *is/are* scheduled for delivery next week.
g The government *is/are* expected to announce new proposals.
h Management *has/have* offered staff a 3% pay rise.
i The news *is/are* on at 10 p.m.
j Police *is/are* investigating fraud allegations against him.
k Their premises *was/were* demolished last year.
l The public *is/are* not interested in the lives of second rate popstars.
m Our swimming team *is/are* the best.
n The United States of America *has/have* been the world's principal economic power.

Vocabulary

5 Which of the topic areas below do the words in the box belong to? Complete the word spiders accordingly. Use your dictionary to help you. The first one has been done for you.

affluence	credit note	consumers	customers
defect	department store	designers	faulty goods
image	Internet	legal rights	lifestyle
mail order	malpractice	money back ·	possessions
retailers	returns	sales assistants	shoppers
shopaholics	status	supermarket	superstore

1

3

2

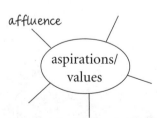

4

6 Which word from the box can precede every word in each group of words below? Use your dictionary to help you decide and check any meanings you don't know.

advertising	brand	consumer
market	retail	shopping

EXAMPLE: awareness, image, leader, loyalty, name
brand (brand awareness, brand image, etc.)

a goods, issues, products, rights, society

b bag, basket, centre, mall, spree, trolley

c agency, budget, campaign, executive, slogan

d forces, leader, niche, research, segment, share, value

e business, outlet, price, therapy

7 Which of these expressions take *right*, which take *wrong* and which can take either? Delete the words which *don't* apply. Use your dictionary to help you and check any meanings you don't know.

EXAMPLE: bark up the ~~right~~/wrong tree

a be in the *right/wrong*

b be the *right/wrong* way round

c be within your *rights/wrongs*

d catch somebody on the *right/wrong* foot

e do the *right/wrong* thing

f get hold of the *right/wrong* end of the stick

g get on the *right/wrong* side of

h get out of bed on the *right/wrong* side

i rub somebody up the *right/wrong* way

j strike the *right/wrong* note

k start off on the *right/wrong* foot

l the *rights/wrongs* and *rights/wrongs* of something

m two *rights/wrongs* don't make a *right/wrong*

8 Complete these sentences using appropriate expressions from exercise 7. The number of missing words is given in brackets.

EXAMPLE: I think I'm ...*within my rights*... to demand a full refund. (3)

a Sara .... her teacher by doing as she was told. (6)

b I don't care about .... the matter – I just want you both to stop arguing. (5)

c She .... by spilling coffee over her boss on her first morning. (6)

d Chris suspects Mark of stealing her watch, but I reckon she's .... (5)

e Your skirt is on .... (4)

f As soon as they met they started to .... and now they don't speak to each other. (7)

g She is very genuine and always tries to .... (4)

Use of English

9 Read the text below and use the word given in capitals at the end of some of the lines to form a word that fits in the space in the same line. There is an example at the beginning (0).

One woman in five is a shopaholic

Retail therapy has become one of Britain's most (0) *pleasurable* leisure	PLEASURE
(1) .... But the percentage of the population suffering from the	PURSUE
serious (2) .... condition of shopping addiction is reaching crisis point,	MEDICINE
(3) .... the number of drug and drink addicts in the UK combined.	TAKE

Experts believe ten per cent of the population, and possibly twenty per cent of women, are manic, compulsive shoppers. Most shopaholics

are (4) .... in debt, and the condition has led to family break-ups,	HEAVY
depression, (5) .... and even suicide.	HOME

Known as omniomania, the condition has been known to psychiatrists since the early 1900s but only now is it reaching epidemic proportions.

Jim Goudie, a (6) .... psychologist at Northumbria University, said,	CONSUME

'One of the reasons behind this sudden rise is that shopping has

never been so (7) .... Shopping centres are beautiful these days,	ATTRACT

absolute wonderlands. Store cards are offered at the till and people

can obtain (8) .... of credit cards with relative ease.'	FIST

Goudie believes shopping addiction masks deeper problems.

'Mostly there is underlying depression and (9) .... Often it can be a	ANXIOUS
disturbed relationship with one's parents. Cold and (10) .... parents	EMOTION

often lavish presents on children and they then come to associate that with pleasure.'

Summary skills

1 Quickly skim through the two texts below to answer these questions.

1 Which text is about
   a a private performance? ☐   **b** a concert performance? ☐
2 Which text is written
   a by the listener? ☐   **b** about the listener? ☐
3 Which text is taken from
   a a newspaper review? ☐   **b** a novel? ☐

Text A

It was the silences that were the most
extraordinary part of Andras Schiff's homage
to Otto Klemperer. What Andras Schiff does
between the notes of Beethoven, Mozart and
5 Haydn is music-making of the very highest
order – elegant, exuberant, chaotic and
sensitive. What he does with the notes
themselves is, of course, simply wonderful.

Wednesday night's concert at the Barbican
10 was one of those occasions when you listen
and think that this is exactly what a concert
should be – risky and revelatory. Schiff's pre-
eminence as a pianist in the classical
Viennese repertoire is well-established, but
15 his strength as a director is more contentious.
For those who believe a conductor should be
in absolute control of each note from every
player all of the time, this could have been a
frustrating experience. But for those who see
20 music as a responsible and responsive
partnership between orchestra and director,
it was heaven.

Under Schiff's elegant, intelligent
direction the smallest details rang clear and
25 the tension between the elements was
maintained on a knife-edge. Music is just
so simple when you pull the pieces apart –
it's only scales and arpeggios and rhythm
and a volume control – but so astonishing
30 when you are forced into really hearing it
by a great musician.

Text B

Pelagia had never before heard such elaborate
virtuosity, and never before had she found a
piece of music to be so full of surprises.
There were sudden, flashing tremolos at the
beginning of bars, and places where the music 5
hesitated without losing its tempo, or sustained
the same speed, despite appearing to halve or
double it. Best of all, there were places where a
note so high in pitch that it could barely be
sounded descended at exhilarating pace down 10
through the scale, and fell upon a reverberant
bass note that barely had had time to ring
before there came a sweet alternation of bass
and treble. It made her want to dance or do
something foolish. 15

She watched wonderingly as the fingers of his
left hand crawled like a powerful and menacing
spider up and down the mandolin. She saw the
tendons moving and rippling beneath the skin,
and then she saw that a symphony of 20
expressions was passing over his face; at times
serene, at times suddenly furious, occasionally
smiling, from time to time stern and dictatorial,
and then coaxing and gentle. Transfixed by this,
she realised suddenly that there was something 25
about music that had never been revealed to her
before: it was not merely the production of sweet
sound; it was, to those who understood it, an
emotional and intellectual odyssey. She watched
his face, and forgot to attend any more to the 30
music; she wanted to share the journey. She
leaned forward and clasped her hands together
as though she were in prayer.

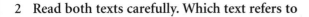

2 Read both texts carefully. Which text refers to

1 the characteristics of a good concert?
2 the effect of the performance on the performer?
3 the role of an orchestra conductor?
4 the effect of the performance on the listener?

3 Read the texts again and, for 1–5, choose which sentence (a or b) more accurately summarises a point from the texts. Underline the relevant points in the texts.

1 a Essentially music comes down to notes, chords, rhythm and loudness, but in skilled hands those components have tremendous power.
   b Essentially music is astonishingly simple when you hear it broken down into its component parts by an expert.

2 a The real power of music lies in what it reveals about the composer's, as well as the performer's, journey through life.
   b The real power of music is its ability to transport the listener beyond the pleasure of the sound on an emotional and intellectual journey.

3 a The power of music can lie as much in the spaces between the sounds as it does in the sounds themselves.
   b The power of music stems as much from the music-making skills of the composer as it does from the way individual notes are struck by the performers.

4 a Careful attention to detail and the balancing of extremes contribute a certain excitement.
   b Clear sound quality and the clever use of disharmony contribute a certain excitement.

5 a Music which is unpredictable in tempo and pitch is surprisingly difficult to listen to.
   b Unexpected variations in pace and range add drama, contrast and appeal.

4 Combine the phrases from exercise 3 into a paragraph summarising the ideas in both texts on what makes music powerful. Think about a logical order of points and any linking words or phrases which might be useful.

5 Try to shorten your summary to between 50–70 words.

Grammar

6 Complete this sentence in nine different ways by choosing the most appropriate ending (a–i) for each verb (1–9). Use each ending once only. You will need to think carefully about form and meaning.

EXAMPLE: 1 e *He might practise in the music room with a bit of encouragement.*

	(1) might practise		a if he hadn't lost the key
	(2) could have practised		b as often as he can.
	(3) should practise		c without first asking permission.
	(4) can't be practising		d as we can't find him anywhere else.
He	(5) should not have practised	in the music room	e with a bit of encouragement.
	(6) must have been practising		f if his teacher hadn't recommended it.
	(7) might not have practised		g – he doesn't have his saxophone today.
	(8) must be practising		h – he only has to ask.
	(9) could practise		i or his things wouldn't still be in there.

7 Complete these sentences using the verbs in brackets with an
   appropriate modal auxiliary from the box. You will need to think
   carefully about meaning and may need to change the form of the
   verbs. Sometimes you will need to use a negative. There may be
   more than one correct answer.

can	could	may	might	must	should

EXAMPLE: He _can't have enjoyed_ (enjoy) the concert – it was terrible!

a Research suggests you .... (score)
   better on a standard IQ test if you listen to Mozart first.

b Strange as it .... (seem), Mozart's music
   .... (have) a profound effect on the brain.

c If you had had a better violin teacher, you .... (give
   up).

d Nobody was impressed by the musicians. They really ....
   (prepare) better for the audition.

e Anyone who's interested in flamenco really .... (go)
   to Spain.

f You .... (still learn) an instrument, you know. It's not
   too late.

g I .... (say) I would go to the concert. I'm really not
   looking forward to it.

h She's listed twice in the programme. She .... (play) in
   both pieces.

i Surely, they .... (both learn) the trombone, can they?

j You .... (pass) your music exam if you had practised a
   bit more.

k Surely he .... (let) them know he was going to be late.

l The show .... (cancel) – it's scheduled to run until
   December.

m She .... (practise) for an hour; she only began 30
   minutes ago.

n The technicians .... (set) the sound system up wrong;
   we couldn't hear the strings at all.

o We were supposed to meet at the stage entrance after the performance. Do you think
   he .... (forget)?

p If you have been living abroad for three years, you ....
   (hear) of him, but I can assure you his music is very popular here now.

Vocabulary

8 One verb collocates with all the words and phrases (1–8) on the left. Use your dictionary to help you work out what it is and choose a meaning for each idiom you make from the definitions (a–h) on the right.

1	offence at	a	accept an argument
2	someone's advice	b	accept them for what they are
3	someone unawares	c	surprise, startle someone
4	pity on	d	be quite difficult
5	something lying down	e	feel hurt by
6	the point	f	follow a suggestion
7	things as they come	g	feel sorry for and help
8	some doing	h	accept something without complaining

9 Hidden in the box are five *adjectives* and five *nouns*. To find them you need to look horizontally, vertically and diagonally in the direction of the arrows. The first one is done for you.

When you have found them, make *adverbs* from the adjectives and *adjectives* from the nouns and combine them to make *adverb + adjective* collocations which you can use to complete the sentences below.

S	U	R	P	R	I	S	I	N	G	R
T	I	F	O	R	P	H	N	B	E	I
R	S	U	T	B	T	I	G	E	D	K
I	U	M	E	E	S	G	H	A	A	V
K	O	T	N	A	H	C	I	T	M	I
I	I	L	T	U	G	N	E	E	A	O
N	V	A	I	T	I	W	D	N	G	Z
G	B	R	A	Y	H	T	S	W	E	A
P	O	T	L	J	W	E	A	L	T	H

Arrows: → ← ↓ ↑ ↘ ↗

EXAMPLE: Considering they lost all their possessions in the fire, they are ~~surprisingly~~ ~~cheerful~~ . *[handwritten: out]*

a No wonder her daughter became a model. She is
....

b Industry bosses are warning that an interest rate rise now is .... to the economy.

c Some people think Hollywood's top film stars are
....

d According to the latest annual report, the company is actually ....

Use of English *[handwritten: round]*

10 For questions 1–6, think of one word only which can be used appropriately in all three sentences.

1 The whole orchestra thinks very
.... of their conductor.
The unexpected finale rounded off a *[handwritten: highly]*
.... entertaining evening's programme.
Given the lack of funds, it seems
.... likely that the concert hall will close.

2 The rain .....*poured*..... steadily on the roof and showed no sign of stopping.
Politeness was one thing my parents really
.....*poured*..... into me as a child.
The chairman was eventually .....*poured*.....
out of office for incompetence.

3 Surely it is better to proceed .....*awhile*.....
than rush in and come unstuck.
Although there was still a long way to go, he was starting to feel ....
optimistic.
.....*awhile*..... opening the door, she took a deep breath before entering the room.

4 The composer's birthplace is commemorated by a large ....
plaque.
The lead violinist had the .....*[handwritten: nel]*....
to ask for a 30% pay rise!
It has long been a dream of theirs to play in the .... section of an international orchestra.

5 The president said that there were no plans to .... taxes in the short term. *[handwritten: get]*
I've been trying to .... Jack over in Tokyo all day without success. *[handwritten: gone]*
The announcement is sure to
.... a loud cheer.

6 He tied the ribbon round the parcel and secured it with a .....*knot*..... .
The audience clapped as he picked up his
.....*knot*..... ready to start playing his violin solo.
There was a distinct .....*knot*..... in the *[handwritten: w]* timber but it was still usable.

Reading

1   You are going to read an article about a popular TV cartoon series. Seven paragraphs have been removed from the article. Choose from paragraphs A–H the one which fits each gap (1–7). There is one extra paragraph which you do not need to use.

The Simpsons

Nick Griffiths meets the faces behind America's best-loved family of cartoon characters

Mike Scully, writer/producer of *The Simpsons*, is in Aspen Colorado with the show's creator, Matt Groening, to attend the four-day US Comedy Arts Festival. Among the attractions is *The Simpsons Live*, a read-through of two separate episodes onstage by members of the cast.

1

The shorts ran from 1987 and were subsequently developed into a full series that made its début on American primetime two years later. From the off, the show was a huge hit, topping Fox's ratings. Although it is hard to figure out why it exploded so quickly, Scully has his own theory.

2

The Aspen venue for the *Simpsons* events is the Wheeler Opera House. The seven-strong cast take the stage, including Dan Castellaneta (Homer Simpson and others), Nancy Cartwright (Bart and others) and Yeardley Smith (Lisa).

3

Stripped of the visual distraction of animation, you also realise how relentlessly clever and funny the scripts are. After the show, Scully acknowledges, 'It's times like that when you realise just what an impact the show has had on people. *The Simpsons* were dysfunctional yet you could also see that they loved and stuck by each other. People have always liked that because they don't see enough of it in real life.'

4

Quite simply, *The Simpsons* redefined television animation, spawning shows that were extreme by comparison – which naturally helped its own acceptance into the mainstream. For every action, of course, there's an equal and opposite reaction. 'Every time there's a fad that kids really like, there's gonna be a grown-up going, "Something's wrong here"', says Groening. 'It happened with video games, heavy metal, rap, and Pokemon.'

5

Indeed, it was deemed so influential that even President George Bush Senior waded in, criticising its portrayal of the American family during his 1992 election campaign. His wife, Barbara, called the show the 'dumbest thing' she had ever seen.

6

Groening refers to his secret motto, 'To entertain and to subvert'. 'It's not so much trying to change the minds of people who are already set in their ways, it's to point out to children that a lot of the rules that they're told are by authorities who do not have their best interests at heart. That's a good lesson. Think for yourself.'

7

But perhaps what pleases Groening and Scully most is the well-known fact that families watch *The Simpsons* together. In an age of meals-on-the-move, three-television households, computer games and the Internet, it is an achievement of which they can be justifiably proud.

mes

strike a chord

A Unwittingly, *The Simpsons* struck a chord, which endures today: however much they mess up and frustrate each other, they are a viable family unit. Yet the American networks misread this popularity as a public craving for more primetime animation. 'They rushed all these shows on air and the public rejected most of them,' Scully explains.

B 'At the core is a family, and everyone can identify with that,' he says. 'This is probably why it plays well overseas, too.' At the last count, the series has been shown in a staggering 94 countries worldwide.

C In a small way, *The Simpsons* probably contributed to the demise of the administration. 'It didn't fly with a lot of Americans,' recalls Scully. 'People who enjoyed the show didn't want to be told that they were watching something bad or stupid, or something wrong for their kids.'

D Serious issues crop up regularly on the show, cloaked in humour and vivid animation: corrupt media and politicians, ineffective policing, the environment. Groening again, 'In conceiving the show, I made sure Homer worked in a nuclear power plant, because then we can keep returning to that and making a point about the environment.'

E So a mere animation series has quietly subverted the world's youth, helped to bring down a president, been stamped all over what we wear and changed the face of contemporary animation. Now academics are using it in universities: *Having the donut and eating it: self-reflexivity in The Simpsons* is part of the Introduction to Cultural Studies module at Edinburgh's Napier University.

F Groening is a chunky, bearded man with tiny specs, a floppy fringe, Simpsons baseball jacket and baggy jeans. Oregon-raised and LA-based since college, he initially conceived the Simpsons family as a brief animated segment within the new Fox TV network's *Tracey Ullman Show*.

G And such was the case initially with *The Simpsons*. Homer was seen as a disgraceful role model; Bart's insolence to his elders would encourage the same. Bart Simpson t-shirts (notably 'Underachiever and proud of it') became so popular that some schools banned them for their subversive messages.

H It doesn't matter that both episodes have been aired previously on television. In the second, Lisa falls in love with the school bully (Bart to Lisa: 'I'll probably never say this to you again, but you can do better'). Watching a short, smiling woman come up with his voice is surreal and deeply impressive.

Use of English

2 Complete the second sentence so that it has a similar meaning to the first sentence using the word given. Do not change the word given. You must use between three and eight words, including the word given.

1 It is absolutely essential to get this parcel off today or we will lose the contract.
 despatched
 This parcel _must be despatched today without_ fail or we will lose the contract.

2 Central Gallery is nowhere near as good since there was a change of ownership.
 downhill
 Central Gallery has really _gone downhill since it was given into another_ hands last autumn.

3 In my youth, cycling 80 kms a day was easy, but I couldn't do it now.
 difficulty
 When I _was a child, ~~there was no~~ I had no difficulty in_ cycling 80 kms a day, but I couldn't do it now.

4 Sarah's mother complained constantly but Sarah had stopped paying attention years ago.
 notice
 Sarah no longer _takes ~~a~~ notice of her mother's_ complaining.

5 Geoff is unlikely to be invited to the wedding given the way he has behaved recently.
 doubtful
 In view of his _recent misbehaviour, it is doubtful ~~proves to if Geoff~~_ be invited to the wedding.

6 They were playing so well, there was no way they would lose the last match of the season.
 bound
 Such was the standard of _match that they were bound to_ the last match of the season.

7 You're so lazy, you don't deserve to pass your exams next month.
 fail
 You're so lazy, it will serve _right if you fail_ your exams next month.

8 Now that their parents have consented to their marriage, their future happiness is guaranteed.
 stands
 Now that they have their _marriage consented, nothing stands in the_ way of their future happiness.

Grammar

3 Complete these extracts with an appropriate participle form of the verbs in brackets.

Take a KODAK with you

The Kodak Girl

While the No 1 Kodak box camera (1) .... (produce) in 1889 was a crucial landmark in the development of photography, two of the most significant cameras in terms of modern photography were the Leica 1 (2) .... (introduce) in 1925 and the Kine Exacta (3) .... (introduce) in 1937, (4) .... (consider) to be the forerunner of sophisticated SLR cameras. First (5) .... (introduce) in the 1950s, meanwhile, the Hasselblad is still the most widely used professional 'work horse' camera, (6) .... (offer) as it does a wide range of specialist accessories. (7) .... (use) to capture the famous Apollo moon-landing pictures, the Hasselblad is also assured of a place in the history of photography.

The son of a printer and keen amateur photographer, Frank Meadow Sutcliffe became best known for his landscape and documentary work, although portrait photography was his living and he was highly acclaimed in this field, (8) .... (win) numerous medals at international exhibitions. One of his best pictures, a group of naked children (9) .... (play) in a boat, is a fine example of his natural almost reportage approach, but landed him in considerable trouble, (10) .... (cite) by the Church as an example of depravity.

One of the most dominant figures in photography, Henri Cartier Bresson's approach is that of the purist, (11) .... (use) the most basic equipment and never (12) .... (resort) to the contrivance of unusual viewpoints or exaggerated perspectives. (13) .... (study) painting, he took up photography seriously in 1931, (14) .... (go on) to exert a tremendous influence on the medium. He insisted that his pictures were not cropped and was at pains to preserve his anonymity. A phrase (15) .... (coin) by him to describe his own approach – 'the decisive moment' – has become the watchword for many thousands of photographers (16) .... (bend) on (17) .... (secure) a winning image.

(18) .... (show) an early interest in the subject, Ansel Adams did not in fact take up photography as a full-time occupation until 1930, (19) .... (open) a gallery (20) .... (specialise) in photography and other arts in San Francisco in 1932. Actively (21) .... (lecture) and (22) .... (teach) in the field of creative photography for most of his career, Adams' contribution to it (23) .... (accept) as a medium of fine art was enormous.

Vocabulary

4 One noun collocates with all these adjectives. What is it? Use your dictionary to help you decide.

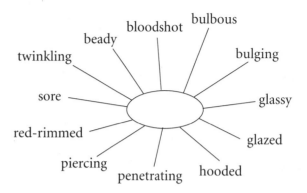

5 The words in capitals in these sentences are all anagrams of verbs meaning *see*. Use your dictionary to help you solve them.

EXAMPLE: Try to RUIPECT yourself lying on a beach in the hot sun.   picture

a I CREEVDIEP a note of unhappiness in her voice.
b I could just INCREDS a figure in the darkness.
c This university has EDISTEWNS quite a few changes over the years.
d The new bridge is an incredible sight to LOHDEB.
e People who are colour-blind can't USTDHISINGI the difference between red and green easily.
f I was so surprised when he turned up – I'd DALEUVSISI someone much older.
g She ENMIDAIG herself sitting in her favourite armchair back home.
h When do you VENGESAI finishing the project?
i He couldn't OCCENIVE of a time when he would not be able to paint.

6 Complete these sentences with appropriate prepositions or particles.

a She never looked .... after that first exhibition.
b I hope things will start to look .... in the New Year.
c She was looking .... seeing the grandchildren again.
d He had looked .... his uncle since he was a child.
e A large crowd looked .... as the band played.
f I'll look .... the reason for the decision.
g The police warned shopkeepers to look .... forged notes.
h I said hello but she looked straight .... me.
i They're looking .... have a meeting within a month.
j I can't come to the whole party, but I may look .... for a few minutes.

Summary skills

1 You are going to read two texts offering an alternative slant on the 'urban jungle'. Before you read, quickly scan through both texts for the information to label the picture and choose the correct headline from page 33 for each text. Ignore the underlining.

1 ....Seagull....

2 ....Wingspan....: about 4ft.

3 Lifespan: ....20 years....

Text A

Their high-pitched cries used to echo around craggy clifftops and they appeared on every seaside postcard. But Britain's hungry seagulls are deserting their coastal colonies and descending on cities far inland in a desperate search for food.
5 Although the overall population is declining rapidly, (1) it is estimated that the urban population of herring gulls and black-backed gulls is rising by as much as 24 per cent a year. In scenes (2) reminiscent of Alfred Hitchcock's terrifying *The Birds*, attacks on humans (3) are becoming increasingly
10 common.

Ian Mitchell, co-ordinator of the Seagull 2000 monitoring project, said: 'There are even some in Birmingham – and that is as inland as you can get.'

The seagulls are attracted to cities (4) because of the easy
15 pickings from landfill sites and the food littering the streets from ever-spreading fast-food outlets. Many seagulls (5) have entirely given up living on or near water and have set up colonies in town centres, on industrial sites, the roofs of supermarkets, and by power stations. More than 10 per cent
20 of all seagulls in Britain are now thought to live on buildings.

David Harry, bird control manager at the pest prevention company Terminix, said: 'They have learnt there is a free and easy source of food in town centres and municipal dumps. They're all born and bred in town centres. Seagull isn't a
25 very good name for them any more.'

Seagulls – who live for up to 20 years and have wingspans of about 4ft – can be very aggressive. There are increasing reports of them attacking people, particularly builders and roof workers. Harry said: 'They get very aggressive when
30 they breed, from late March to early August. They dive-bomb people and actually strike them. They take ice-creams and fish and chips from people's hands.'

Recently a builder rendering a wall in Cardiff was attacked and ended up with stitches. People have also been
35 attacked in Wiltshire, and one person fell off a roof trying to fight off seagulls.

Text B

Terrifying scenes reminiscent of Alfred Hitchcock's (6) horror film *The Birds* have been occurring on the Côte d'Azur (7) in recent months as flocks of aggressive seagulls have begun attacking tourists and residents in some of the world's most famous resorts. 5

The gulls, which ornithologists say are (8) exceptionally large, have swooped on people, pets and other birds. The most notable attack took place when a woman out walking her Yorkshire terrier in Monaco was left in a state of shock after two enormous specimens 10 descended on the small dog, lifted him up in their beaks and carried him out into the harbour where they dropped him in the sea and devoured him. One elderly woman in Nice called the fire brigade when her balcony was invaded by dozens of aggressive gulls after she fed one. 15

The attacks are causing concern to city councillors from Nice to Monaco. Experts say the number of gulls has increased 50-fold in the region over the past decade. 'This is happening because they (9) have a great capacity to adapt, are extremely opportunist and with their strength 20 and size, are able to (10) take precedence over other species of birds. They just won't accept any competition,' said Philippe Ewald, an ornithologist with the Museum of Natural History in Nice.

Along the Côte d'Azur the birds have also found a 25 paradise where food abandoned by tourists provides easy pickings for the scavengers.

'They have got so much to eat that they are reproducing without any problem,' said Dr Alain Moussu, a Nice vet who is president of the region's 30 League for the Protection of Birds. Gulls are a protected species in France and so cannot be culled.

Seagull army invades inland towns

Bird-bites-dog shock as towns go gull crazy

2 Read Text A. Why does David Harry say: 'Seagull isn't a very good name for them any more.' (lines 24–25)?

3 Read Text B. What reference does Text B share with Text A? Why do you think both writers have used it?

4 Read both texts again and think of ways to shorten or paraphrase the underlined sentences or phrases. Check your ideas against these options (a–j).

  a by the accessibility of food
  b dominate
  c are growing
  d now live exclusively in built-up areas
  e oversized
  f recently
  g suggesting
  h numbers of city-based gulls could be growing
  i thriller
  j are highly adaptable

5 Find individual words in the texts with these meanings. The paragraph number is given in brackets.

Text A
  a leaving without intending to return (1)
  b places where birds nest together in groups (1)
  c making continuous observations (3)
  d insect or animal which is destructive (5)
  e places where refuse is unloaded and left (5)

Text B
  f groups of birds travelling together (1)   *flock*
  g popular holiday centres usually on the coast (1)   *resorts*
  h experts specialising in the scientific study of birds (2)
  i examples of a particular group or class (2)
  j looking for ways to gain an advantage (3)
  k scientific group of animals or plants (3)
  l state of perfect happiness (4)
  m animals or birds that search for and feed on waste (4)
  n reduced in number through selective killing (5)

6 Which of these points are made in Text A, which in Text B and which in both? Tick the boxes which apply. The first one is done for you.

	Text A	B
a seagulls are leaving their traditional habitats	✓	
b seagulls are moving into towns		
c seagulls are descending on coastal towns		
d seagulls are colonising inland towns		
e seagulls are noisy		
f seagulls are thriving on the ready supply of food in towns		
g seagulls eat food dropped in the streets by visitors		
h seagulls eat food left on rubbish dumps		
i seagulls eat food dropped in the streets by fast-food customers		
j seagulls have established successful colonies in towns		
k there are 50 times the number of seagulls that there were 10 years ago		
l numbers of urban seagulls are increasing dramatically		
m the total number of seagulls is falling		
n the culling of seagulls is prohibited		
o seagulls are aggressive birds		
p some seagulls are oversized		
q seagulls are attacking humans		
r attacks on humans are increasing		
s seagulls are attacking locals and visitors		
t seagulls pose a particular threat to outdoor construction workers		
u seagulls have started attacking domestic animals and other birds		
v seagulls are particularly aggressive during their breeding season		

7 Write two or three sentences summarising the reported changes in seagull behaviour and their impact, using the points in exercise 6 to help you.

Use of English

8   For questions 1–15, read the text below and think of the word which best fits each space. Use only one word in each space. There is an example at the beginning (0).

Early civilisations, like the later (0) ....*ones*......... , seem to have a common positive characteristic in (1) .... they change the human scale of things. (2) .... bring together the cooperative efforts of larger numbers of men than any earlier societies and usually (3) .... this by physically bringing (4) .... together in larger agglomerations, too. (5) .... the word 'civilisation' suggests, it is usually marked (6) .... urbanisation. Admittedly, it would be a bold man (7) .... was willing to draw a precise line at the moment when the balance tipped (8) .... a dense pattern of agricultural villages clustered (9) .... a religious centre or a market to reveal the first true city. (10) .... it is perfectly reasonable to say that more (11) .... any other institution the city has provided the critical mass which produces civilisation and that it has fostered innovation better than any other environment so (12) .... Inside the city, the surpluses of wealth produced by agriculture (13) .... possible other things characteristic of civilised life. They provided for the upkeep (14) .... a priestly class which elaborated a complex religious structure, leading to the construction of great buildings (15) .... more than merely economic functions, and eventually to the writing down of literature.

Grammar

9   Rewrite these sentences starting with the word(s) in brackets.

EXAMPLE: The minute the mayor walked into her office, the phone started ringing. (No sooner)

No sooner had the mayor walked into her office than the phone started ringing.

a   The traffic ground to a halt just after they joined the freeway. (Scarcely)
b   The council only started showing interest in the redevelopment scheme last month. (Not until)
c   These are by far and away the most imaginative proposals the city has ever received. (Never before)
d   Government investment in public transport is often not remotely adequate. (Seldom)
e   The new transport network had not long been open when a number of similar schemes were announced in cities around the country. (Hardly)
f   The only other time I have seen such deprivation was in slums that are now demolished. (Only once)
g   It is very difficult for town centre redevelopments to achieve a harmonious balance between old and new. (Rarely)
h   After the minister had finished his tour of inspection, he made his pronouncement. (Only after)

10   Rearrange these words to make meaningful sentences. The first word of each sentence is correct.

EXAMPLE: Around city's core boulevard a fine intact medieval the runs wide.

Around the city's intact medieval core runs a fine wide boulevard.

a   So becoming more seeking stressful cities more life and that alternatives is people some in are.
b   Under take own circumstances matters residents their should into no hands.
c   Little chairman to signed was land desk petition 50,000 was on a by his aware the that people about.
d   Here sturdy town stood of fortifications once the the.
e   On property account will you everything tell no believe should developers you.
f   Not further way only already unemployment a problem also losses job was on were the but.
g   Such crime leaving residents could impact was the they area the if of that were in.
h   In jeopardise scheme want no of did success they way to the the.
i   Not development councillor one the accepted the view invitation to.
j   Little demolition quickly neither did did expect to the she and start I so.

Vocabulary

11 Complete these extracts with words from the boxes.

built	development	divisive	favour
greenfield	ill-planned	problem	transit

air	commuting
driving	flow
infrastructure	job
road-users	hour
transport	

America has convinced me that too much space for urban (**1**) .... is a bad thing. When humans are pressed they come up with creative solutions – Manhattan is an outstanding example of a great city (**2**) .... within a 12 × 3 mile plot. Where (**3**) .... expansion is endlessly possible, the results are ugly, (**4**) .... and socially (**5**) .... Above all , such developments (**6**) .... the car, and even Americans are coming to see that the car is a (**7**) .... and not a solution. Minneapolis has just started work on its first mass (**8**) .... system.

architecturally	demand	economy	housing
pressure	prove	reinvent	populated

As everyone knows, the Netherlands is one of the most densely (**9**) .... countries in the world. At the same time, it has a healthy (**10**) .... and there is a (**11**) .... for moderately priced (**12**) .... The (**13**) .... on land is very great, as is the need to (**14**) .... ways of using it. The situation has allowed young architects to (**15**) .... themselves. The result is that the Netherlands is at present one of the most (**16**) .... vital of countries.

After little investment in (**17**) .... for 25 years, California's (**18**) .... system is groaning. Businesses complain about potential employees turning down (**19**) .... offers that would compel them to spend hours a day (**20**) .... Car makers worry that unless (**21**) .... quality improves they will be ordered to meet yet stricter design standards.

Road-pricing has long been championed by economists, keen to impose more of the external costs of driving on (**22**) .... by charging them a fee that reflects not just the distance travelled but also the time and route of the journey. (**23**) .... imposes a heavier burden when it is done at rush (**24**) .... so such journeys ought to cost a driver more. In theory, drivers will then adjust their departure times and smooth out the (**25**) .... of traffic through the day.

Reading

1 For questions 1–18, read the three texts below and decide which answer (A, B, C or D) best fits each gap.

Fined – for not taking a passport to the lavatory

For eight years, Leonid Dobronogov has crossed the Russian–Ukrainian border a dozen times a day without ever leaving home.

Mr Dobronogov has the bad luck to be the owner of a house and garden that has the border running (1) .... it. When it was all part of the Soviet Union, it did not make much (2) .... , but now he lives in two separate, (3) .... countries simultaneously. If he does not want to be fined by the local customs officers he has to carry a passport every time he pays a visit to his outside lavatory.

Mr Dobronogov may be the unluckiest resident of Uspenskaya, but he is not the only one who has been forced to pay the 'fines' (4) .... by the ever-vigilant border guards stationed at the (5) .... of the village. The customs officers stationed there (6) .... scan through binoculars the main road through the village along which the border runs. Residents crossing the invisible line are fined if they are not carrying their passports.

1 A along	B through	C up	D over
2 A trouble	B exception	C inroad	D difference
3 A sovereign	B impartial	C constitutional	D disunited
4 A foisted	B imposed	C impressed	D commanded
5 A boundary	B fringe	C edge	D margin
6 A recurrently	B continually	C continuously	D interminably

The Dance of Anger by Harriet Goldhor Lerner

Do you find yourself always fighting with your nearest and (7) .... , distancing yourself through silence, or blaming others for the failure of your relationships?

For so many women anger is a destructive force which (8) .... all the harmful dynamics of our most intimate relationships. In this inspirational book, renowned feminist Harriet Goldhor Lerner draws on a decade of clinical investigation, as well as recent findings in psychoanalytic theory, to show how all women, regardless of age, background or experience, can (9) .... anger into a constructive force.

Focusing largely on the family, this book (10) .... the reader with the insights and practical skills to stop (11) .... in the old predictable ways – and begin to use anger to establish a more positive approach to significant relationships.

Harriet Goldhor Lerner is a psychologist and psychotherapist. Her work on the psychology of women and the management of anger has earned her international (12) .... among general and professional audiences.

7 A closest	B sweetest	C best-loved	D dearest
8 A perpetuates	B perpetrates	C promotes	D persists
9 A control	B turn	C alter	D form
10 A provides	B affords	C offers	D gives
11 A following	B falling	C behaving	D enacting
12 A notoriety	B awareness	C reputation	D recognition

The Quiz: How happy are you?

1 Which of the following most accurately describes your income and expenditure?
a) You are constantly in the (13) .... and you despair of ever having enough money.
b) You have more than enough to buy the basics, and can afford to buy yourself regular treats.
c) You have to be careful with money, but are no (14) .... than anybody else.

2 Thinking back to the last major traumatic event in your life, did you
a) (15) .... it gradually, through introspection and the support of friends/family?
b) seek professional therapeutic help?
c) take a (16) .... of anti-depressants or other medication to alleviate the distress?

3 You apply for a more senior position in your company, but the post is advertised and filled by an outsider. What do you do?
a) feel angry and decide to look for a similar position elsewhere
b) (17) .... yourself with the thought that you would have hated the added responsibility anyway
c) resolve to work harder and devote more time to your professional (18) ....

13 A black   **B red**   C pink   D blue
14 A harder off   B well off   C worse off   D worst off
15 A get over   B get through   C go over   D go through
16 A course   B treatment   C dose   D cure
17 A Reward   B Treat   C Remind   D Comfort
18 A approach   B promotion   C ambition   D development

(handwritten margin notes: blood; red; Little ... did she kn...)

Use of English

2 Complete the second sentence so that it has a similar meaning to the first sentence using the word given. Do not change the word given. You must use between three and eight words, including the word given.

1 Puzzle-solving is one of her favourite pastimes and always has been.
passion
She .... *has been puzzle-solving* .... *since* .... she was a child.
(handwritten: has had a passion)

2 Do you mind if I don't come back to the office after I've been to the dentist at lunchtime?
afternoon
Would you have any .... *objection to me taking the afternoon* .... off after my dental appointment?

3 They all agreed that the new dress code was a complete success.
hailed
The new dress code .... *was hailed as a complete success by* .... everyone.

4 Everyone knows you are not allowed to smoke on domestic flights these days.
prohibited
It is common *knowledge* .... *known that it is prohibited to smoke* .... on domestic flights these days.

5 She knew nothing of her husband's impending promotion.
about
Little .... *she knew about her husband was ... to* be promoted.

6 He can't possibly have said anything like that.
misheard
You really .... *had to misheard him* .... completely.

7 She only ever has one chocolate at a time.
permits
She never .... *permits herself more to* .... one chocolate at a time.

8 Such attention is quite unusual for a contemporary work of art.
receive
Seldom .... *does receive a contem ... receive* .... quite such attention.

Vocabulary

3 Which of these characteristics from the Chinese zodiac are negative? Use your dictionary to help you decide. Some may be a matter of opinion!

The Horse	athletic eloquent entertaining gifted hard-working independent quick-witted ruthless selfish unfeeling
The Goat	dissatisfied insecure irresponsible lovable peace-loving pessimistic sweet-natured undisciplined unpunctual
The Monkey	enthusiastic inventive long-winded passionate unfaithful untruthful untrustworthy witty
The Rooster	amusing boastful conservative extravagant industrious mistrustful pedantic pompous short-sighted vivacious
The Dog	courageous cynical devoted introverted modest noble prosperous respectable selfless stubborn
The Pig	gullible honest loyal materialistic naïve non-competitive scrupulous sensitive sincere sociable

4 Match the signs to these descriptions, underlining the characteristics in the table above that justify your answers.

EXAMPLE: They are funny, lively and hard-working, but they can also be a bit suspicious, self-important and full of self-praise.

> *Rooster – amusing, vivacious, industrious, mistrustful, pompous, boastful*

a Honourable, brave and well-to-do, they tend to attach easily to people and put others first, but they can be inward-looking and a bit obstinate.

b A bit innocent and easily taken in, they like the fine things in life and pay attention to detail. Very genuine, they enjoy being among people and will always stand by their friends.

c They are amusing, eager people who are good at thinking things up, but they can be unreliable and may not always tell the truth.

d They are kind and gentle people, easy to love, but not always easily pleased. They sometimes lack confidence, often have an underdeveloped sense of responsibility and can't always look on the bright side.

5 Add an appropriate prefix to make the opposite of these adjectives from exercise 3. Use your dictionary to help you.

EXAMPLE: <u>un</u> sociable

a ....enthusiastic
b ....honest
c ....loyal
d ....modest
e ....noble
f ....selfish
g ....sensitive
h ....sincere

6 Find the six compound adjectives in exercise 3 and use the *first* word of each to complete these sentences. Use your dictionary to help you. There may be more than one correct answer.

EXAMPLE: Some parents have a lot to put up with but are extremely ....long........-suffering.

a The affair may have been very public but it was very ....-lived.

b The councillor's ....-hitting remarks at the meeting upset a lot of people.

c The Finance Director is renowned for being rather ....-tempered in a crisis.

d At election time, you will find .... - talking politicians everywhere.

e In any confrontation, her brother always adopts a ....-keeping role.

7 Which prefix can attach to every word in each list below? Use your dictionary to help you decide and check any meanings you don't know.

EXAMPLE: bearing, joyed, wrought

> *over (overbearing, overjoyed, overwrought)*

a conscious, literate, skilled
b disposed, eminent, possessing, occupied
c dated, going, raged, ranked, standing
d assured, centred, important, opinionated, satisfied, styled

Grammar

8 Gerund or infinitive? Complete these sentences with an appropriate form of the verbs in brackets. There may be more than one correct answer.

EXAMPLE: They decided *to put off tidying* (put off/tidy) the house until their visitors had left.

a She stopped .... (iron) her clothes and started .... (put) them away.

b He regretted .... (take) the job when he found he couldn't stand .... (work) with his new boss.

c The new recruits all promised .... (improve) their standard of dress at work.

d Apparently, no-one minds her .... (be) so untidy round the house. Her housemates don't like .... (be) tidy themselves!

e They managed .... (defuse) the situation and .... (avoid/get) caught up in an ugly scene.

f We meant .... (practise/do) the yoga exercises but the director objected to us .... (use) the room.

g Having advised him .... (embark) on a course of therapy, the counsellor went on .... (suggest) that he try .... (see) a few different therapists before choosing one to work with.

h Until she heard his voice, she had forgotten .... (meet) him three years ago.

i 'Remember .... (stay) calm, whatever happens!' she shouted after him.

j You've let your house .... (get) in a terrible state. There's no point .... (try/clean) it yourself – you'd better .... (get) a professional cleaner in.

k The kids are at an age now where they want .... (be allowed/do) what they want, not .... (be made/ do) what we want them .... (do).

l I was hoping .... (buy) a new outfit for the occasion, but my bank manager's forbidden me .... (spend) any more money!

m Predictably, he denied .... (lie) to them about the theft.

n I've only found two things worth .... (read) in this newspaper.

o He's been meaning .... (phone) you for a couple of weeks now.

9 Circle the correct options in italics to complete this text. Sometimes more than one option is correct.

Put *a little spirit* into your work

Does your company offer you the chance (1) *de-stress / to de-stress / de-stressing* with t'ai chi or yoga classes at lunchtimes? An on-site vicar with whom you can discuss those concerns of work (2) *take / to take / taking* over your life? An afternoon philosophy workshop on ways (3) *bring / to bring / bringing* 'soul' into the office? If not, it may only be a matter of time. Spirituality is set (4) *become / to become / becoming* the biggest workplace fad of the millennium.

Law firm Mishcon de Reya was among the first companies (5) *get / to get / getting* employees involved. 'We sponsored a poet in residence who conducted seminars for everyone from secretaries to senior partners,' says a spokesperson. 'All employees agreed that (6) *write / to write / writing* and (7) *analyse / to analyse / analysing* poems helped (8) *create / to create / creating* an environment where 'deep' issues could be explored and then transferred to workplace matters. In turn, that broke down barriers and improved staff morale.' Words are the tools of a law firm's trade, explains the spokesperson. 'So (9) *try / to try / trying* (10) *think / to think / thinking* about other, more spiritual, areas, where words are equally important, seems the perfect way in which (11) *enhance / to enhance / enhancing* our working environment.' Rob Briner, an organisational psychologist who specialises in the link between work and well-being, agrees: 'It is finally being recognised that we need (12) *appeal / to appeal / appealing* to employees' hearts and souls as well as to their minds and pockets.'

UNIT 10 Globalisation

Summary skills

1 Quickly read through Text A and Text B, ignoring the gaps, and decide which headline belongs to which. Where do you think the texts are from?

A COMMITMENT TO REDUCE INEQUALITY

Globalisation – a positive force for all

Text A

What is globalisation? **(1)** .... , it means that today, more than ever in the past, groups and individuals interact directly across frontiers, without necessarily involving the state. This happens **(2)** .... because of new technology, and **(3)** .... because states have found that prosperity is better served by releasing the creative energies of their people than by restricting them.

The benefits of globalisation are obvious: faster growth, higher living standards, new opportunities. **(4)** .... a backlash has begun. Why? **(5)** .... these benefits are very unequally distributed; **(6)** .... the global market is not yet underpinned by rules based on shared social objectives; and **(7)** .... , if all of tomorrow's poor follow the same path that brought today's rich to prosperity, the earth's resources will soon be exhausted. **(8)** .... the central challenge we face today is to ensure that globalisation becomes a positive force for all the world's people instead of leaving billions of them behind in squalor.

If we are to get the best out of globalisation and avoid the worst, we must learn how to govern better at local and national levels, and to govern better together at the international level. We must think afresh about how we manage our joint activities and our shared interests, **(9)** .... many challenges that we confront today are beyond the reach of any state acting on its own.

That does not mean world government or the eclipse of nation states. **(10)** .... , states need to be strengthened. **(11)** .... they can draw strength from each other by acting together within common institutions based on shared rules and values.

Text B

In Delhi, a bicycle rickshaw driver has a mobile phone pressed to his ear. In Mauritius, a buyer from GAP examines the latest fashions in shirts. In a London hospital, a pathologist inspects the blood sample of a tourist for signs of malaria. Troops from a dozen different countries try to keep the peace in Sierra Leone. **(12)** .... in Amsterdam, experts from around the world negotiate the price at which pollution from American factories could be traded for lower coal consumption in developing countries.

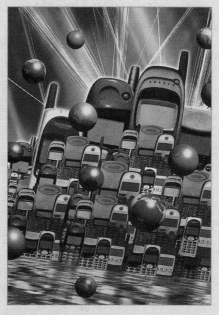

This is what globalisation has already brought us. Global communications. Global commercial opportunities. **(13)** .... some worrying global problems. Just one decade of the Internet has shown us how quickly information, ideas and capital now spreads across the globe. Imagine another 50 years of growth in the technology and in the use of it. Everyone on earth will share an interest in global free trade, cheap global communications, a clear global environment and sustained global peace.

Globalisation will bring huge rewards for some, **(14)** .... it does carry risks: **(15)** .... , the risk that we will not manage it equitably. Rich and powerful countries will be the first to capture the benefits. **(16)** .... they can take little comfort in their own prosperity, if poverty and disease grow unchecked elsewhere.

(17) .... , the international development targets for 2015 are really rather modest. Do we have to wait till then to halve the scale of world poverty? **(18)** .... to get every child into primary school?

2 Read both texts again and decide where in the texts these words belong.

> **Text A**
> and
> essentially
> on the contrary
> thus
> because (× 3)
> for
> partly (× 2)
> yet

> **Text B**
> against that background
> above all
> but (× 2)
> and (× 2)
> or

3 Without looking back, decide which of the following are seen by the writers as challenges facing a global world. Then read the texts again to check and make some notes on the points that apply.

   a to maximise the economic benefits of globalisation and make sure they are shared equitably
   b to work together socially and politically
   c to make technology accessible to more people
   d to combat pollution, war, poverty and disease
   e to make education universal

4 Using your notes from exercise 3 to help you, summarise in your own words as far as possible the challenges facing a global world according to both texts. Try to write between 50 and 70 words and use two or more linkers from the list.

of primary importance   on the one hand ... on the other
not only ... but also   in addition

Use of English

5 For questions 1–6, think of one word only which can be used appropriately in all three sentences.

1 To get your message across effectively, you need to think carefully about the .... you use.
However furious you are, there is no excuse at all for .... like that.
If there was just one .... in the world, do you think we would communicate any better?

2 .... mineral deposits are one of the country's major resources.
Eating a .... meal late at night can give you indigestion.
It's a bit .... to talk about globalisation when half the human race has yet to use a phone.

3 She turned the .... and pointed excitedly to her destination.
The environment conference attracted people from around the ....
.... artichoke served with melted butter is one of my favourite foods.

4 The main thing that struck us about the report was the .... of ideas.
The .... of the soil is a major factor affecting the region's ability to feed itself.
Around three billion people live in .... and the number is increasing.

5 Is it really .... for a business like yours to stay open 24 hours a day?
Many of the world's nations are in a very poor .... state.
In the face of recession, the Government's .... policies have come in for a lot of criticism.

6 Many global companies now .... around the clock.
Changes are being introduced to make the department .... more efficiently.
In view of the seriousness of the case, surgeons decided to .... immediately.

Grammar

6 Complete these sentences with an appropriate form of the verbs in brackets. You will need to think carefully about form and meaning. Sometimes you will need to add *would*. There may be more than one correct answer.

a At times like this, I really wish we .... (speak) Japanese!

b She wishes .... (enrol) for a language course as soon as possible.

c I wish you .... (try) to get to grips with the Internet. I'm sure you .... (enjoy) it.

d If only the good things in life .... (be) free!

e I wish new technology .... (not keep) changing all the time.

f If only we .... (have) a mobile phone at the time, we .... (be able) to call them.

g She .... (pass) her exam last year, if only she .... (work) harder.

h He behaves as though he .... (be) the only caring person on the planet.

i If only globalisation .... (be) a positive force for all.

j If only we .... (not agree) to go with them that day.

k He was acting as though he .... (be) in a desperate hurry.

l Would you not rather they .... (seek) new sponsors than see the programme abandoned?

m It is time .... (start) taking the world's problems seriously.

n He wished more research .... (do) while the language still .... (have) speakers.

o I'd much rather you .... (ask) permission before helping yourself.

p They had hoped .... (move) the project on further before their funding .... (run) out.

Vocabulary

7 Complete this extract with words from the box.

beneficial	development
disempowers	employment
forces	globalisation
harnessed	higher
inequality	integration
nations	poverty
technological	transport

The word '(1) ....' stirs powerful emotions. Some see it as highly (2) .... – a key to future world economic (3) .... , more opportunities and (4) .... living standards across the world. Others see it as a malign force that increases (5) .... within and between (6) .... , (7) .... the weak, threatens (8) .... and living standards, and increases (9) ....

Most people agree that the (10) .... driving globalisation – (11) .... change, lower communication and (12) .... costs, increased trade and financial (13) .... among countries – are powerful. But they need to be (14) .... to make globalisation work for the good of all.

8 Using each preposition in the box twice, make an appropriate phrasal verb or noun with *turn* for each picture. Use your dictionary to help you.

down	in	off
over	out	

EXAMPLE: to turn somebody in

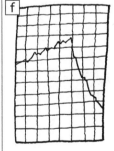 a

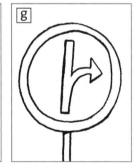 b

 c

 d

 e

 f

g

 h

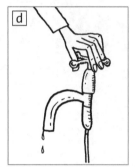 i

9 Complete these sentences, which all contain expressions with *turn*, using your dictionary to help you.

a Beside herself with emotion, she didn't know which .... to turn.

b Everyone agreed her redundancy was a very unfortunate turn of ....

c Goodness! You .... me quite a turn creeping up like that!

d She is so kind. She'll do anyone a .... turn.

e It's bizarre. Since I joined the programme, I seem to meet him at .... turn.

f The coast road is so full of .... and turns, it's really quite dangerous.

Reading

1 You are going to read an article about relationship problems at work. For questions 1–7, choose the answer (A, B, C or D) which you think fits best according to the text.

Fighting talk

It would seem that some people are simply incapable of settling scores amicably at work and practising some good old-fashioned forgiveness. A high court judge was recently forced to order two doctors who were unable to settle a personal dispute to divide their surgery in two by building a wall right through their medical practice.

You might think that doctors Anne Rodway, 65, and Paul Landy, 49, were old enough to know better but somehow the two could not manage to work alongside each other. The two set up their partnership three years ago in Sevenoaks, Kent, but stopped talking just three months after their business started. Both staff and around 3,500 patients have been asked to decide on which side their loyalties lie as the practice is formally divided – especially difficult for the staff, who have already had to become used to being paid separately by the warring doctors.

Although an extreme case, it demonstrates just how bad things can get when communication and understanding breaks down between colleagues at work. Office feuds can be experienced in even the friendliest of environments. But what to do when faced with one?

Whether you are involved directly or an innocent bystander watching others curdle the workplace atmosphere, Jane Clarke, author of *Office Politics*, offers some sound advice. 'On the whole, people do not like dealing with conflict, but it is very important to grab the bull by the horns. If you feel you are able to, you should try and sort it out. If not, the very least you can do is report it to a manager who should make sure that workers know that bad behaviour in the workplace will not be tolerated.'

But what causes acrimony in the first place? Reasons can be as diverse as a clash of personalities, jealousy, backstabbing or a simple misunderstanding. Whatever the cause, there has to be a strong desire to solve the problem if things are to get better. If you are personally involved – and almost all of us have been in one way or another – then the best thing to do, says Clarke, is to try to put yourself in the other person's shoes. Easier said than done, since empathy is not an easy emotion to come by, even to the most virtuous.

'Often it is easy to dump on the other person and blame them totally for the situation but remember it is your problem and you have a responsibility to try to resolve it,' says Clarke.

Listening skills are vital. If the problem is between other colleagues, things can be a bit trickier. You may not be the gallant sort – practising an unhealthy dose of denial is often what most people would prefer to do – but ignoring the situation will not make it go away.

So what are your options? 'If you feel you are up to it, try talking with the feuding parties individually and try to understand what the issue is,' advises Clarke. 'Make it clear that it is not an acceptable state of affairs.'

Mediation is another option; get the two parties to sit together and act as a buffer zone. You might have the urge to bash their heads together, but it

won't be terribly constructive. As Clarke says, 'Sometimes it is a case of translating. People are often so different that it seems that they speak a different language.'

Any meetings between disputing colleagues should have some follow-up. All involved should be made aware of the next steps – failing to do this could mean that the situation repeats itself.

Negative energy between people need not produce bad karma. Harnessed creatively, it can actually become a positive force. So, if you are having problems with office dullards who insist on putting downers on any bright new ideas you might have, use their criticism and objections as a way of really testing a brainwave. Surely, if it can survive them, it can survive anyone. Try looking at people's weaknesses as strengths: assign a pedant to research the finer details of a project; the loudmouth of the office can always be pushed forward when it comes to public speaking.

Disputes and ill feelings can arise both among employees or between employee and employer, a fact clearly illustrated by the record numbers of people who contacted the conciliation service ACAS over the past year. Reassuringly, however, 76% of cases were settled through mediation – an indication, perhaps, that rather than working on building walls in the workplace, we should be bringing them down.

1 In telling the story of the two doctors, the writer suggests they
   A didn't give their partnership enough of a chance.
   B were totally incompatible from day one.
   C should have been able to resolve their problems.
   D were introverted and intolerant people.

2 What main point is the doctors' story used to illustrate?
   A Conflicts at work divide staff and clients.
   B The failure of relationships at work can have serious consequences.
   C Work conflicts can happen where you least expect them.
   D It is not always easy to know how to handle conflicts at work.

3 What is Jane Clarke's advice to anyone caught up in an office dispute?
   A Seek appropriate advice.
   B Get in touch with your feelings.
   C Write a report to your manager.
   D Take appropriate action.

4 According to Jane Clarke, office disputes
   A occur for any number of reasons.
   B are caused in the first instance by acrimonious feelings.
   C are usually attributable to personality differences.
   D are rarely the result of office politics.

5 Work conflicts will not get resolved unless both parties
   A have a personal involvement.
   B accept the blame for the situation.
   C want to find a solution.
   D are willing to change places with each other.

6 What does *them* (line 69) refer to?
   A problems
   B office dullards
   C downers
   D bright new ideas

7 Which of the following best describes the style of the article?
   A constructive and straightforward
   B detached and critical
   C understanding and empathetic
   D ironic and dismissive

Grammar

2 Which of the adverbs in italics are correct? Sometimes both options are correct, sometimes neither option is correct. Delete the incorrect options and, if neither option is correct, suggest a suitable alternative.

    EXAMPLE: All three couples seemed ~~entirely~~/*very* pleasant and ~~absolutely~~/*eminently* suitable as foster parents.

  a The new receptionist is *immensely/deeply* grateful to you for putting in a good word for her with her boss.

  b There was something *deeply/absolutely* mysterious about her, which he found *extremely/rather* attractive.

  c In this day and age, it is *utterly/entirely* unusual for couples to get married, let alone stay together 'till death them do part'!

  d The line managers say the proposed pay rises are *woefully/fairly* inadequate and *grossly/absolutely* unfair.

  e New technology may be *absolutely/completely* marvellous, but developing a good working relationship with it can be *extremely/pretty* challenging!

  f The new Finance Manager was *really/eminently* upset by the MD's remarks. We all felt they were *pretty/quite* hostile and not *entirely/quite* reasonable.

  g My new boyfriend finds my father *rather/utterly* intimidating, but Dad's actually *completely/quite* harmless.

  h She's *highly/woefully* old now, but still *quite/really* determined to be independent.

  i He's *fairly/absolutely* devoted to his cat. It's *utterly/immensely* hopeless trying to change him now!

Vocabulary

3 Which of the suffixes in the box can be used to make adjectives from these verbs and nouns? Use your dictionary to help you write in correct adjectives. Don't forget to indicate any possible negative forms using prefixes!

-able	-ary	-ible	-ical	-ive	-ous	-some	-ful	-less

  a argue    (un)arguable, argumentative

  b awe

  c defend

  d fear

  e forget

  f imagine

  g moment

  h rest

  i sense

  j use

4 Use adjectives from exercise 3 to complete these sentences.

EXAMPLE: At this stage, it is ....*arguable*.... which of them is more to blame for the problems in their relationship.

a It is quite .... how much some people are capable of achieving in life.

b She may have been extremely upset with him, but her behaviour was quite ....

c Starting a new life alone after years of marriage is a rather .... prospect for any new divorcee.

d I've noticed I'm becoming more and more .... these days. I must be getting old!

e We need to be sure that their grievances are real and not ....

f What do you think was the most .... discovery of the eighteenth century?

g Both parties were becoming .... waiting for the mediation proceedings to begin.

h That's utterly absurd. I've never heard anything quite so .... in my whole life!

i Sadly, their efforts to work out their problems were .... They've gone their separate ways.

5 Match these adverbs and adjectives to make appropriate collocations and use them to complete the sentences below.

blindingly	banal
comparatively	biased
deceptively	rare
heavily	obvious
highly	questionable
radically	simple
ridiculously	reformed
utterly	cheap

EXAMPLE: The fact that she's having an affair with her boss is ....*blindingly obvious*.... to everyone except her husband.

a It is .... whether these goals can be achieved within the time available.

b A book this old in such good condition is a .... find these days.

c The research they based on a so-called 'random' sample of couples turned out to be .... in fact.

d The plan sounded .... Whether it would prove so in practice was another question, however.

e You can count on her to come out with some .... remarks!

f The 20th century saw many national institutions ....

g £25 is .... – there must be something wrong with it.

Use of English

6 For questions 1–15, read the text below and think of the word which best fits each space. Use one word only in each space. There is an example at the beginning (0).

How can you tell if you'll stick it (0) ......*out*...... with your partner and grow old together or whether, (1) .... some corner down the road, (2) .... is an acrimonious and expensive break-up waiting? It seems that luck and determination may not be the (3) .... factors involved. Pinning (4) .... exactly how and why people (5) .... in love, and whether they are likely to (6) .... a success of life together is a subject that is exercising the skills of scientists around the world. In the US, relationship analysis is a well-developed science. Nearly 50 per cent of American marriages (7) .... in divorce, (8) .... is costly both (9) .... material and emotional terms. American research institutes want to know why this happens, and (10) .... can be done. (11) .... of the best-known is the Family Research Laboratory at the University of Washington, aka the Love Lab. The Love Lab is run by Dr John Gottman PhD, (12) .... believes that he is able to distinguish happy relationships that will (13) .... the test of time from unhappy (14) .... that will crash and burn – (15) .... an accuracy rate of 90 per cent.

Summary skills

1 The two texts are about the same scientific discovery. Quickly read through them, ignoring the underlining, to find the answers to these questions.

  a Which scientist is mentioned by name in both texts? What is his position?

  b Which phenomenon is referred to by name in both texts? What is it?

  c Which bacterium is mentioned by name in both texts? Where is it found?

Text A

A 'Lazarus' bacterium which thrived **(0)** <u>millions of years before dinosaurs walked the Earth</u> has been brought back to life. Biologists are astonished that the 250 million-year-old bug could be revived, suggesting that if conditions are right, bacterial spores might survive indefinitely.

  It also adds weight to the controversial notion that life was scattered through the cosmos by comets. The theory, put forward in 1981 by astronomer Fred Hoyle, suggests that comets 'seeded' life on Earth.

  Provisionally named *Bacillus permians* to denote the geological period from which it originates, the born-again bacterium is unknown to science. 'It is alive and, to the best of anyone's knowledge, **(1)** <u>there's no other organism that's been around that long</u>,' says Russell Vreeland, the scientist who isolated the bacterium. **(2)** <u>Its nearest 'ancient' rivals</u> are bacterial babes by comparison, just 25 to 40 million years old.

  Vreeland and his colleagues at West Chester University in Pennsylvania isolated the ancient bacterium from the Salado salt formation at Carlsbad, New Mexico, an underground cavern used for storing nuclear waste. While the salt crystals were forming **(3)** <u>250 million years ago</u>, bacterial spores in a drop of water became trapped **(4)** <u>in a cavity in the</u> salt – a feature known as an inclusion. Geologists dated the layer where the crystal was found – 560 metres down in a shaft leading to the repository – at 250 million years old.

  (5) <u>Under scrupulously sterile conditions</u>, Vreeland liberated the spores from **(6)** <u>their hibernation</u>. He **(7)** <u>extracted the 3-microlitre inclusion</u> and **(8)** <u>squirted it onto growth medium</u>. The spores grew into familiar rod-shaped bacillus bacteria. Vreeland is now comparing the genes of the ancient bug with those of two **(9)** <u>contemporary relatives</u>: *Bacillus marismortui*, from the Dead Sea, and *Virgibacillus pantothenticus*.

  John Parkes, a geomicrobiologist at the University of Bristol, says that survival of such ancient spores is astonishing. 'All the laws of chemistry tell you that the complex molecules in the spores should have degraded to very simple compounds such as carbon dioxide,' he says.

  Parkes says that before people start jumping to conclusions, they should wait until someone else finds similar bacteria from the same salt formation. But if it is proven that spores can survive this long, he wonders, why should they die at all? 'Where else are these dormant organisms waiting to be reawakened?'

Text B

A quarter of a billion years ago, back in the Permian era, a vast inland sea covered much of west Texas and south-eastern New Mexico. As the outlet linking this sea to the ocean became blocked, the sea began to evaporate slowly, leaving behind the mineral and saline deposits of the so-called Salado Formation. Russell Vreeland and William Rosenzweig, biologists at West Chester University in Pennsylvania, with their colleague Dennis Powers, a geologist, started analysing Salado salt crystals in the hopes of finding some biological record of this bygone time. Together they found what could be the world's oldest surviving life forms.

Trapped inside the crystals of rock salt were tiny drops or 'inclusions' of brine, capable of serving as perfect biological time capsules from the Permian era – provided they had not been contaminated since. The researchers' most pressing concern, therefore, was to establish that the crystal samples, and their precious cargo, had remained intact since their formation. By using stringent sterilisation procedures, the researchers satisfied themselves that modern bacteria had only a billion-to-one chance of slipping into their ancient samples. Then, after carefully drilling a hole into the crystals' walls and removing the few microlitres of fluid from each inclusion, the researchers began testing their samples for life.

Of the 66 inclusions examined, three showed evidence of viable bacteria. So far, the biologists have characterised just one of these strains. It is a spore-forming bacterium, dubbed 2-9-3, which came from a crystal that was retrieved from the wall of an underground shaft in New Mexico. Through DNA sequence comparisons, Dr Vreeland established that 2-9-3 was 99% identical to a modern species called *Bacillus marismortui*, which has recently been shown to inhabit the brackish waters of the Dead Sea. Both 2-9-3 and its modern cousin appear to have adapted for survival in their respective salty homes.

But 2-9-3 is able to tolerate salinity only to a certain extent. When its surroundings grow too salty, it forms spores and waits until conditions improve. Indeed, this seems to be the key to its longevity. Dr Vreeland speculates that, as the Permian sea dried out, 2-9-3 retreated into its spore, where it survived comfortably, encrusted in salt, until aroused from its suspended animation 250m years later. (The previous record for longevity was held by another bacterium, which was revived after 25m years, after being extracted from an extinct bee trapped in amber.)

2. Underline phrases in Text B which echo the underlined phrases in Text A.

EXAMPLE: **(0)** A quarter of a billion years ago, back in the Permian era

3. Find single words in the texts with these meanings (which text is given in brackets).

EXAMPLE: brought back to life (A + B)
revived

a identified and separated (A)
b access tunnel (A + B)
c place of storage (A)
d temporarily inactive (A)
e rendered impure (B)
f capable of developing and surviving independently (B)
g salt content (B)

4. Now use your own words to summarise what is said in both texts about the Salado Formation and why it is of interest. Write between 50 and 70 words.

Grammar

5. Complete the sign explanations below using an appropriate verb from the box in the passive with a modal if necessary. There is sometimes more than one correct answer.

expect	extinguish	integrate	keep
leave	park	permit	remove
reserve	switch off	wear	

EXAMPLE: Cars ...*may be parked*... free of charge but vehicles and their contents ...*are left*... entirely at the owners' risk.

a Eye protection .... at all times.
b All cigarettes .... before entering this area.
c All fire exits .... clear and free of rubbish.
d Mobile phones .... before entering this concert hall.
e No unauthorised persons .... beyond this point.
f This space .... for disabled parking only. Unauthorised vehicles ....

6 Complete these extracts with the correct passive form of a verb or verb + adverb from the box.

allow	already find	deal (× 3)	link
sprinkle	suspect	think	

Every newborn baby (1) ....
a genetic hand of cards which helps to determine how long he or she
(2) .... to play the game of life. There are good cards, which predispose those who have them to a long and healthy existence, and there are bad cards, which predispose people to high blood pressure, say, or heart disease. Occasionally, cards (3) ....
out that doom their holders to an early and debilitating death. In the past, people never knew exactly which cards – in other words, which genes – they (4) ....
.... They could guess at the future only by looking at the kind of health problems experienced by their parents or grandparents. Genetic testing, which makes it possible to probe for dangerous genes, has changed all this.

Clouds at the centre of the Milky Way (5) ....
with sugar, astronomers have shown. They say the finding could help them home in on complex interstellar molecules that may have given rise to life on Earth.

The chemical make-up of interstellar clouds (6) ....
.... to be similar to that of gas clouds in the vicinity of the early Earth, and could help explain how biological molecules came to be present on Earth so soon in its history. More than a hundred simple organic molecules, including methanol and acetic acid, (7) .... in space.

A mass stranding of whales and dolphins in the Bahamas
(8) .... to underwater noises made by the US Navy. Marine mammal specialists who examined the animals say that haemorrhages in and around their ears suggest that they become disoriented after a very loud noise. While low-frequency naval sonar (9) .... of harming whales in the past, this is the first time mid-level frequencies, commonly used by battleships, have attracted attention.

Vocabulary

7 Hidden in the box are 12 verbs. To find them you need to look horizontally, vertically and diagonally in the direction of the arrows. The first one is done for you. When you have found them all, think of one verb which they could all be said to mean.

A	Z	R	**D**	K	C	A	H	→
H	E	C	**I**	L	S	C	S	←
S	T	E	**S**	I	C	X	E	↓
A	R	T	**S**	K	U	R	V	↑
L	A	C	**E**	R	A	T	E	↙
S	N	I	**C**	W	R	I	R	
G	O	H	**T**	I	P	L	B	
B	O	I	**N**	C	I	S	E	
P	T	R	**I**	M	W	A	S	

8 Complete these sentences using each verb from exercise 7 once. You may need to change the form of the verb.

EXAMPLE: The man's face was severely <u>lacerated</u> in the accident.

a A programmer has managed to .... into some top-secret government data.

b He .... open the envelope with a knife.

c My hair grows so fast, it needs .... again already.

d In biology classes at school we used to .... rats.

e The museum was broken into by vandals again last night and several paintings were ....

f Could you .... me a very thin piece of cake?

g The design is .... into a metal plate.

h She's .... and changed jobs for as long as I've known her.

i He was .... away at his violin, making a terrible noise!

j Although his hand was completely .... , surgeons have been able to sew it back on.

k During the operation, the surgeon .... several tumours from the wall of the patient's stomach.

9 Complete these sentences with appropriate prepositions. Prepositions may be used more than once and there may be more than one correct answer.

EXAMPLE: Apparently he was really cut ......up...... ...about.... the research grant being withdrawn.

a It's time this engine had a service. It keeps cutting ....
b They were hoping a good talking to would cut her .... size.
c Although she came from a wealthy family, she was cut .... without a penny.
d It's a problem that seems to cut .... all strata of society.
e As funds start to get low, we may have to cut .... lab time.
f He doesn't think twice about cutting .... , no matter who you are talking to.
g The bandage was so tight it was starting to cut .... the circulation.
h Have you finished cutting .... the templates yet?
i She was so angry she cut the cheque .... lots of little pieces.
j Three more trees would have to be cut .... before the site was cleared.
k It's quicker if you cut .... the park.
l There's an awful lot of red tape to cut .... before we get the project up and running.

Use of English

10 Read the text below and use the words given in capitals at the end of some of the lines to form a word that fits in the space in the same line. There is an example at the beginning (0).

Just how (0) ......readable.......... should a popular science book be? This may seem   READ
an odd question, but there is an important issue at stake here, as was made clear
at the recent Aventis Science Book Awards, when jury chairman Lewis
Wolpert (1) .... espoused the cause for making the genre more   PASSION
demanding of readers.
    The biologist believes too many science writers are now running scared of
(2) .... As he pointed out, the public does not expect James   COMPLEX
Joyce or T.S. Eliot to be easy to follow. Indeed, readers positively relish these
authors' intricacies, (3) .... excesses and abstruse metaphors. So   LABYRINTH
why then do we exclude science writers from such (4) .... , Wolpert   EXPECT
asked. Why do we presume that they – and only they – adopt the approach of
the lowest common literary denominator and grind down the infinite
(5) .... of the universe to an easy-to-digest pap?   SUBTLE
    In short, science books should be written to produce as much cerebral sweat
as do *Ulysses* and *The Wasteland*, a point (6) .... by his jury's   EXEMPLAR
choice of winner – Brian Greene's long, dense and extremely technical *The
Elegant Universe*, an (7) .... treatise on cosmology.   COMPROMISE
    And it is here that we reach the nub of the issue for, although elegantly written,
the book is of such density and (8) .... it pushes the notion of   OPAQUE
popular science writing close to the precipice of (9) .... and leaves   COMPREHEND
one fearful that it will only daunt, rather than attract, the (10) ....   INITIATE

Reading

1 You are going to read four extracts which are all concerned in some way with the environment. For questions 1–8, choose the answer (A, B, C or D) which you think fits best according to the text.

Dhole (*Cuon alpinus*) Size: Head and body length, 90cm; tail, 43cm Weight: 17kg
Habitat: Forests and scrublands throughout Asia Surviving number: Unknown
Photograph by Anup Shah

WILDLIFE AS CANON SEES IT

Dholes, also known as the red dog of Asia, are highly social animals. When chasing prey through dense forest, pack members keep in contact with each other with a unique whistling sound. Like the endangered African wild dog, dholes have been relentlessly persecuted, and although now protected in some areas, they continue to be threatened by habitat loss, disease and reduction of prey.

To save endangered species, it is vital to protect their habitats and understand the role of each species within the earth's ecosystems. As a global corporation committed to social and environmental concerns, we hope to foster a greater awarness of our common obligation to ensure that the earth's life-sustaining ecology survives intact for future generations.

Digital Plain Paper Copier
The GP55 provides high-resolution reproduction and versatile image editing with Canon's exclusive Digital Image Processing System, while offering comprehensive capabilities for networked document management with the optional Multi-Device Controller.

Canon

Canon is supporting the UNEP International Photographic Competition on the Environment 1994-1995

AT GAP INC'S OFFICE COMPLEX IN SAN BRUNO, California, planes fly low overhead, on their final descent into San Francisco's international airport. But for the 600 employees who work there the polluting crates are but a distant rumble, drowned by birdsong from the more natural winged creatures living in the building's grass roof.

The complex is constructed along industrial ecology lines, a revolution in industrial design and architecture that is gathering pace across the world. Even manufacturing giant the Ford Motor Company is planning a major overhaul of its largest plant which will revolutionise the way it makes cars, all under a grass roof.

The roofs of the Gap complex, which uses 30 per cent less energy than the maximum permitted by law, are planted with native grasses and wild flowers atop six inches of soil. They act as a thermal and acoustic insulator, almost obviating the need for air conditioning – and they absorb the greenhouse gas carbon dioxide.

High ceilings, huge atriums and interior courtyards bring natural light deep into the buildings.

---

1 Why do dholes feature in this advertisement?
  A They are unusual in the way they interact.
  B They have developed their own means of communication.
  C They are related to Africa's endangered wild dogs.
  D They are at risk of potential extinction.

2 Which of the following best summarises Canon's underlying message?
  A Canon wants to see Asia's dholes protected and off the danger list.
  B Canon wants to see more research into individual species and ecological issues.
  C Canon is a responsible company that wants to play a part in preserving the planet.
  D Canon is a company that knows about wildlife and the environment.

3 Why is the Ford Motor Company mentioned in the second paragraph?
  A as an example of the spreading industrial design revolution
  B as an example of a large US manufacturer from a different sector
  C as a company interested in revolutionising its production processes
  D as a company that has recently reviewed its production facilities

4 Which of the following is not mentioned as a direct benefit of a grass roof?
  A good soundproofing
  B natural temperature regulation
  C carbon dioxide absorption
  D good natural light

More than a quarter of the world's coral reefs have now been destroyed and nearly three-quarters are likely to be gone within 50 years, a startling new international study says.

line 6 The report, by the official Global Coral Reef Monitoring Network, is the most alarming yet on the fate of the richest and most beautiful celebrations of life in the seas. Although corals cover only one-fifth of 1 per cent of the area of the oceans, they are home to one-quarter of all their species.

The report documents how the reefs of 93 countries – living entities built over centuries by tiny creatures – are being destroyed by over-fishing, pollution, global warming and tourism.

The United Nations Environment Programme, one of the international bodies that established the monitoring network, has set up a Coral Reef Unit to tackle the crisis. Professor Klaus Töpfer, its executive director, said: 'Coral reefs may be the equivalent of the canaries in coal mines, giving early warning that the world's ecosystems can no longer cope with growing human impact.'

Since the time of the Incas, the Chipayas Indians have gathered and traded salt from the sparkling Uyuni salt plains high in the Bolivian Andes. Created 10,000 years ago when a lake the size of France dried up, it forms the oldest and largest salt crust on the planet. At 3,700 metres above sea level, in temperatures of 40°C, the sun's reflection can burn the eyes in minutes.

Strange salt sculptures and the workers cast the only shadows across the baking plain. The Chipayas break the salt crust with simple spades, chiselling out small striped blocks to be loaded onto llamas that carry them down to the valleys of Argentina and Chile. There, like generations before them, they trade the salt for staples of cocoa, pepper, corn and honey. The caravan is this isolated community's lifeline. Before it leaves the village on the edge of the salt flats, a llama is sacrificed, part of a ceremony seeking protection from the goddess of the Earth, Pachaman, for the animals and men on their hazardous journey. It is not only the harsh environment that threatens their existence.

From the valleys below come other Bolivians, who harvest the vast expanse of natural mineral in a semi-industrial way. Some rake huge tracts, others cut massive symmetrical blocks from the multicoloured, layered crust, which they load onto trucks, far more reliable than the llamas.

5 Why is the report *the most alarming yet* (line 6)?
A It states that coral reefs have now disappeared.
B It has found that coral reefs represent less than 1 per cent of ocean area.
C It concludes that reefs are disappearing very rapidly.
D It had access to more data than previous reports.

6 In Professor Töpfer's opinion
A coral destruction is less important than what it symbolises.
B coral is important as a global ecological indicator.
C coral reefs are no different from other living species.
D the world's ecosystems are set on a path to destruction.

7 What is unique about the Uyuni salt plains?
A They have been worked by Chipayas Indians since the time of the Incas.
B They have existed longer and extend further than any other salt plains.
C No other salt plains are as high or as remote.
D No other salt plains are as hot or as inhospitable.

8 In the third paragraph, the writer is suggesting that
A the natural rhythm of the Chipayas' lives is likely to be changed for ever.
B the Chipayas' way of life depends on the salt plains being theirs to work exclusively.
C no part of the world is likely to be safe from encroaching industrialisation.
D the Chipayas' way of life depends on animals that are not always reliable.

Grammar

2 Use these frameworks to rewrite the quotes below in reported speech. There may be more than one correct answer.

EXAMPLE: A leading conservationist says ....
(that) one of the greatest challenges facing the future of rhinos in both Africa and Asia is maintaining sufficient conservation expenditure and effort in the field.

a Industry consultant William Moore acknowledged ...... , but said ....
b Harold Barrington, a recycling enthusiast from Oklahoma, said .... He claimed .... Apparently, he ....
c Liz Newman, a mother of three, mused ...... and she sometimes wondered .... She concluded ....
d Recycling specialist David Dougherty questions ...... , when .... He insisted .... He reckoned .... In his view, people .... But they ....

EXAMPLE:

'One of the greatest challenges facing the future of rhinos in both Africa and Asia is maintaining sufficient conservation expenditure and effort in the field.'

a 'Recycling paper will never completely eliminate cutting down trees, but it could mean cutting fewer trees.'

c 'We live in a world surrounded by concrete and sometimes I wonder what I can do about the environment. Well, I can sort my trash.'

b 'I've built a machine that makes petroleum out of old tyres. I've produced as much as 1,800 gallons of crude oil in five hours. I distilled some into gasoline to run my machines and sold the rest to a refinery.'

d 'Why cut down a tree to make a newspaper with a lifetime use of just over 20 minutes, then bury it? You can use it six times over, then burn what's left to create energy. We've got to make recycling a natural part of the economy so that it becomes a part of our lifestyle. Of all the environmental concerns that have come up through the years, this is the most personal. People are uncertain what they can do about saving whales or the rain forest. But they can recycle their waste every day of their lives.'

Vocabulary

3 Match a word from the left with a word from the right to make 10 common collocations that are useful for talking about the environment. Which are 'bad' for the environment and which are 'good'? Use your dictionary to help you.

1	climate	a	growth
2	concerted	b	pollution
3	endangered	c	gases
4	environmental	d	depletion
5	global	e	species
6	greenhouse	f	lobbyists
7	ozone	g	waste
8	population	h	warming
9	recycled	i	change
10	water	j	action

4 Solve the anagrams in capitals to make a second word with a similar meaning to the first, and decide which word pairs can be used to complete the sentences below.

a	backing	PROSPUT
b	banned	DESHOIBAL
c	chuck	CIRDASD
d	destruction	TAVOASTIEND
e	dosh	EYNOM
f	green	ETERVALNIOMNYLN-YEFDRILN
g	hounded	DESCRUTEPE
h	fix	PRAIRE
i	native	SGINDEOUIN
j	rubbish	FRESUE
k	save	CROPETT

EXAMPLE: The council has given its full ...a.... to the new flood defence proposals.

1 The .... of the world's rain forests is a real cause of concern.
2 Gap's new office complex is incredibly ....
3 I do wish people wouldn't just .... litter in the street.
4 Some people feel bullfighting should be ....
5 It's vital that we work together to .... endangered species.
6 Kangaroos and koalas are both .... to Australia.
7 The rangers at the park have to be able to .... their own vehicles.
8 Please ensure all household .... is ready for collection by 9 a.m.
9 Many species of wild animals have been .... to the point of extinction.
10 You couldn't lend me some .... till I can get to the bank, could you, Ken?

Use of English

5 For questions 1–15, read the text below and think of the word which best fits each space. Use one word only in each space. There is an example at the beginning (0).

Win some, lose some

Britain's biological profit-and-(0) ....loss.... account is in (1) .... black. It stands at around 154 confirmed extinctions over the past century, (2) .... could be closer to 1,000 (3) .... the tiniest insects and fungi are finally taken (4) .... account. Compare this with the upwards (5) .... 1,500 introductions, invasions and new discoveries, estimated by the Joint Nature Conservancy Council. But while it is generally agreed that there are (6) .... arrivals than departures, does this healthy-sounding net increase represent a gain? The answer, (7) .... reasons that do not conform (8) .... the laws of balance sheets, is that it almost certainly does (9) ....

Looking at our native wildlife through the profit-and-loss account is to discover that one of the great unquestioned 'goods' of (10) .... time – biodiversity – is not always a good thing. We have acquired more species, but (11) .... are usually aggressive global colonisers. We are losing the species that made these islands distinctive, the natural communities (12) .... have been here for (13) .... to 12,000 years.

(14) .... so, there are degrees of extinction. Global extinction is the irrevocable one, a permanent minus against the planet's biological resources. National extinction is an indication of environmental damage in our own country, a shame for (15) .... but not necessarily a tragedy for the species.

Use of English

1 You are going to read two texts on health. For questions
1–4, you need only give short answers. For question 5,
write a summary according to the instructions.

evangelical

I realise I'm in danger of coming across
line 2 as evangelical about oily fish, such as
mackerel, tuna, sardines and herrings,
but they have so many positive
nutritional qualities that it's hard to
know where to start. Their benefits to
health are primarily due to their fish-oil
content, specifically omega 3 and 6
fatty acids, which encourages the liver
to produce high-density lipoprotein
(HDL), or 'good' cholesterol, which
works to remove low-density lipoprotein
(LDL), 'bad' cholesterol, from the body.
Because LDL is deposited in the blood
vessels and can cause heart attacks,
angina or strokes by obstructing them,
boosting your intake of HDL can reduce
the risk of developing heart disease.

a lot of
a plethora

Oily fish are also rich in vitamin A,
which is essential for growth, healthy
skin and hair, good vision and strong
tooth enamel. In addition, oily fish give
the body a good dose of vitamin D,
which works in conjunction with calcium
to build healthy bones and teeth.

Although concerns have been raised about the levels of
dioxin that they contain, it appears that the benefits of eating
oily fish far outweigh the potentially slight risk to health of
consuming small amounts of this pollutant.

Oily fish are both impressively versatile and provide a
plethora of health benefits. Not only should you eat them, but
I advise that you introduce your children to them as soon as
you can, giving them small amounts at a time and perhaps
disguising the taste. If you do so, you'll be building up their
bodies to lead a healthy life.

1 In what context is *evangelical* (line 2) usually used and why
is it appropriate here?
2 What contrast is the writer making in the third paragraph?

Girls are storing up health problems for the future because they do not get enough exercise when they are young, says Neil Armstrong of the Children's Health and Exercise Research Centre at the University of Exeter. He says that by the age of 5 or 6, girls already exercise less than boys.

The chief problem is that parents are far too protective of girls, Armstrong told a conference on women's health at the Royal Society of Medicine in London this week. 'It's certainly not a physiological reason,' he says. 'Even at crawling age they're allowing boys to be more adventurous than girls.'

Mayer Hillman, a researcher at the Policy Studies Institute in London, agrees that girls are over-protected. In a study of children under 12, Hillman found that only 1 in 9 girls is allowed out alone during the day, compared with 1 in 3 boys.

line 23   'Parents overreact by restricting their children,' says Hillman. The risk of children being abducted is tiny compared with the risk of developing heart disease because of the lack of exercise, he says.

As well as letting them out more, says Armstrong, parents can persuade children to exercise more by setting a good example. 'What surprised us is how perceptive the kids are about how much their parents do,' he says. For example, if mum takes the

line 33   lift instead of the stairs, he says the kids will notice and follow suit.

3 Explain in your own words how parents *overreact* (line 23).
4 What does the writer mean by *follow suit* (line 33)?
5 In a paragraph of between 50 and 70 words, summarise in your own words as far as possible the advice given in both texts on how parents can help minimise the risk of heart disease in their children.

Grammar

2 Circle the correct preposition or particle and insert the appropriate article (*a, an, the*, or — if no article is required) in the gaps.

a .... research carried out by .... Institute of .... Respiratory Medicine *at/in* .... Royal Prince Alfred Hospital *at/in* Sydney, Australia, suggests that there is .... correlation *between/with* the consumption *in/of* oily fish and .... reduction *in/of* children's risk *at/of* developing .... asthma. New studies are also beginning to make .... connection *between/with* a deficiency in .... omega 3 fatty acids and .... depression and .... mental illness.

b Jane Clark is .... state-registered dietician and .... author *for/of* the *Bodyfoods* series of .... books. As .... teenager she was interested *in/to* medicine but wanted to work *at/with* food instead of .... drugs, so she did .... degree *in/of* dietetics *in/at* Leeds University.

c Everyone responds differently *to/with* food *in/on* the morning: some people feel sleepy and unable to function *on/after* eating .... large breakfast, whereas others need .... hearty breakfast before they embark on .... day's activities.

d .... chocolate causes your blood-sugar level *for/to* rise quickly, which stimulates .... pancreas to produce .... insulin, ... hormone that rapidly brings it *down/under*. .... fresh fruits give .... best slow-release energy boost, so increase your fruit intake.

e .... strenuous exercise results *in/to* .... release *of/with* .... endorphines in .... brain, giving athletes .... natural 'high'. Some athletes become dependent *on/to* .... effect, but it does not harm them *in/by* any way.

f Make sure that you drink plenty of .... water throughout .... day to enable all .... energising vitamins, minerals and slow-release sugars *in/of* the food that you eat to be absorbed *by/through* your body. .... adults should aim *at/to* drink two to three litres of .... water .... day.

g It is best to exercise every day. Three days .... week is .... absolute minimum. Work out .... best time of .... day to fit in .... exercise programme. It is unwise to exercise if you are injured or if you have any form of .... fever or .... viral infection such as .... cold or .... flu.

Vocabulary

3 Replace the verbs in italics with a more neutral verb that has the same meaning and fits in the sentence. There may be more than one correct answer. Use your dictionary to help you.

a The new manager came with a reputation for *shirking* his responsibilities.

b The relay team would continue *striving* for the record.

c Pedro *pleaded* for another chance to play for the team.

d The coach has *shunned* them completely since they *abandoned* his club.

e Francesca *resolved* to *confront* them about the missing equipment.

f 'Can I *lure* you away from your work-out for a minute?'

g We *trawled* through the programme to find out when we were competing.

h Lara always was one to *relish* a challenge!

i It seems they *trounced* the competition to cross the finish line in record time.

j If the pain *persists*, you should *consult* a doctor.

k The government has *pledged* more money for health promotion.

l The doctor *urged* him to take up some form of exercise before it was too late.

4 Using the clues in the picture and your dictionary if necessary, complete the sentences opposite with an appropriate idiom. (The number of missing words is given in brackets.)

EXAMPLE: They may be the latest thing, but these training shoes cost an arm and a leg! (5)

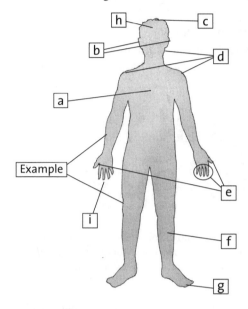

a After worrying about the problem for two months, she was glad to .... (5)

b Could you come back later? I'm .... in work at the moment. (4)

c To be honest, the thought of diving from the high board .... (6)

d She's always been good at swimming. She's .... the others at the club. (4)

e I'm .... this morning. That's the third time I've dropped my chart. (4)

f Did you really win the marathon or are you just .... ? (3)

g Working with people half your age certainly helps to .... ! (5)

h This application form defies the imagination – I can't .... it at all! (4)

i It takes the coach hours to get the sports hall ready, but the players never .... to help him. (3)

Use of English

5 Read the text below and use the word given in capitals at the end of some of the lines to form a word that fits in the space in the same line. There is an example at the beginning (0).

As a teenager, Joe Decker was an (0) ...overweight... couch potato. He devoured | WEIGH
beer, pizza and Twinkies, took no exercise and saw his weight balloon.
When he joined the US army, his (1) .... to run two miles in | ABLE
16 minutes meant he had to endure the (2) .... of extra training | HUMILITY
in the 'fat boy programme'.

Yet Joe Decker has been named the world's fittest man after completing the most gruelling physical challenge on earth in a record time. Scarred by
(3) .... jibes about his weight, 30-year-old Decker is now | END
enjoying the title bestowed on him by Guinness World Records, 'the work-out king of the world'. Where once he had layers of (4) .... blubber, | WANT
now he has lean, honed muscle.

Chris Sheedy of Guinness World Records said: 'His (5) .... is | ACHIEVE
momentous, (6) .... , superhuman. When his letter arrived | BELIEF
I thought, 'to do all this in such a short time isn't physically possible'. But
he sent us videos, eyewitness (7) .... , doctors' reports – | STATE
more evidence than we needed to (8) .... his claim.' | VALID

Always looking for new ways of testing his limits, Decker has experienced hallucinations, (9) .... , dehydration, tunnel vision, extreme | ORIENT
(10) .... , and mind-numbing tedium during races lasting up | TIRE
to a week at a time.

Reading

1 You are going to read an article about gender and the division of labour. Seven paragraphs have been removed from the article. Choose from paragraphs A–H the one which fits each gap (1–7). There is one extra paragraph which you do not need to use.

Men can't help it; blame their biology

I think a nine iron for this one...

In an ideal world men would be women. They would be home-makers and child-minders, cooks and cleaners, unabashed by wearing an apron. They would even use those 'baby-changing stations' that now forlornly decorate public toilets in airports and motorway service areas.

1

Which is not say the new man does not exist. You see him toting the baby on his back, or filleting the kiwi fruit for his partner's supper. However, the new man's most salient characteristic is his rarity. If he had feathers, he would be an endangered species.

2

So, are men just behaving badly? Or is there another reason why they shy away from the iron? Ironing a shirt does not call for extraordinary skill, and men living on their own manage it perfectly well, so why do they shrink from the duty when they are married?

3

'Men are more susceptible to boredom,' says Professor Marvin Zuckerman, an expert on neurotransmitters. 'What happens when you don't get variation stimulation? What happens when there is nothing changing, nothing novel?

It's an unpleasant feeling. Not quite anxiety or depression, dissatisfaction. Men are more impatient and, when they're bored, they find different ways to express their boredom.'

4

Except, of course, for the problem of serotonin. 'It all became routine, mundane, boring. You start to feel: "I did that yesterday, so why should I do it again today?" And then you start to think, "Well, I won't do it today. I'm not bothered today." And then it just deteriorates from there.'

5

The differences are visible in brain-scans. When a man does a crossword puzzle, only the left side of his brain is active, but a woman's brain lights up like Blackpool. She uses both sides of her brain while she solves the clues. And what is true of verbal challenges is true to much of life. Studies show that, in general, the male's brain is focused while hers is more integrated.

6

Last year an experiment was set up to test Fisher's findings. Six men and six women were challenged to complete a series of tasks in a limited time. They had to wash up, brew coffee, make toast and scrambled eggs, iron a shirt and take a phone message. The result was a walkover for the women.

7

Kevin and Lisa finally declared their experiment a failure. 'When Kevin went back to work it was as though a burden had been lifted, he was so chirpy,' Lisa says. Kevin feels he is back doing what he should be. 'We get on much better now I'm at work because I come home and I'm satisfied for the day. I've done my work, I've done a good job,' he says. So you can be a new man, if that is what you want – but only by undergoing a sex change. Easier, perhaps, to wear an unironed shirt?

A 'The female's brain is architecturally designed to do several things at once, whereas the male brain is more focused, more compartmentalised, more built to do one thing after another,' says Helen Fisher, an anthropologist who is also studying the brain. 'And, of course, the home is a place where you need to do a lot of things all at once – like clean the loo, answer the telephone, defrost the peas, feed the dog, change the baby and iron the shirts.'

B Biology, that's why. The culprit is a neurotransmitter called serotonin. We all have it in our brains, but men have less of it, and the less serotonin you have the more impatient and impulsive you are. Serotonin acts as a braking system on our impulses. It placates. It permits us to endure routine and boredom. And men are serotonin-challenged.

C All surveys of household responsibilities show that men are stubbornly resistant to their new role as house-husbands, though interestingly the newer the relationship the more pliant he is. But once he has his boots firmly under her table he becomes the old brute once again – only 2 per cent of men in stable relationships help with the washing and ironing.

D It's not hard to imagine – there's no financial reward and there's certainly no glamour; there's precious little job satisfaction and not much to look forward to from one day to the next except more of the same. But the role of the housewife is different today and, more importantly, so are society's attitudes towards it.

E Take Kevin Beck and Lisa Bates. They fell in love. They married. Each was on their second marriage and each had two children and, because Lisa was on a fast-track career, they agreed that Kevin would be the house-husband. 'I've always looked after myself,' he says, 'and I thought that I could manage. I'm pretty tidy so I thought the house would be as neat and tidy as I want it. I thought it should be a breeze.'

F And it is not just multitasking. Studies also show that from early childhood males have a greater tolerance for dirt. They do not see the stains on a bath or the dust on the bookshelves. Males also have a different sense of smell. He does not detect many of the pheromone-related odours (smelly socks, sweaty shirts) of which women are acutely aware. He sees sweetness and order where she sees filth and decay.

G However, as men cannot be women we have had to settle for the next best thing: the 'new man'. His specifications were dreamt up by feminists who rigorously refuse to recognise any innate differences of aptitude or attitude between the sexes.

H The house got messier as Kevin's low boredom threshold rebelled. Blouses got burnt instead of ironed as his brain strayed in search of diversions. However it was not only serotonin that was crippling Kevin's good intentions. The brains of the male and female are organised in different ways, and this organisation is not an accident of upbringing or culture – it is hard-wired into the cells from conception.

Vocabulary

2 Which word in these groups is the odd one out? Why? Use your dictionary to help you decide.

 a bored, laborious, mundane, routine, tedious
 b assignment, chore, drudgery, duty, task
 c go-getting, high-flying, high-powered, quick-witted, well-appointed
 d contentment, fulfilment, remuneration, satisfaction, stimulation
 e dull, humdrum, indifferent, monotonous, repetitive

3 Which adjective relates to which picture? If you don't know, guess before you use your dictionary to check your answers.

aquiline	bovine	canine	elephantine
equine	feline	porcine	ursine

a *ursine*
b *feline*
c *bovine*
d *canine*
e *aquiline*
f *elephantine*
g *porcine*
h *equine*

4 Complete these sentences using appropriate adjectives from exercise 3.

 a She's so tiny she makes me feel ...... *elephantine* ......
 b The portraits showed an aristocratic family with long ...... *equine* ...... faces.
 c She's very attractive and those green ...... *feline* ...... eyes of hers are particularly bewitching.
 d He was a gentle, rather ...... *bovine* ...... man.
 e The dentist thinks she may now need treatment on two of her ...... *canine* ...... teeth.
 f You can tell he's his father's son by that distinctive ...... *aquiline* ...... nose of his.

Grammar

5 Match the two halves of these sentences. You will need to think carefully about meaning.

 1 He goes into work early on Mondays
 2 He left the office by the fire escape
 3 He was desperate to hide his mistake from his boss
 4 I agreed to her suggestion
 5 I always take an umbrella to work
 6 I deliberately didn't have breakfast
 7 I never finish work until I've cleared my desk
 8 I warned them you'd be late
 9 In order to make the right decision
 10 Leave the keys out
 11 She took a taxi
 12 They were afraid to complain
 13 You'd better take some money
 14 You really should have a back-up plan

 a for fear of getting lost.
 b for fear (that) it would jeopardise his promotion.
 c in case things don't work out the way you want.
 d in case you find you need some.
 e in order not to upset her.
 f in order to plan his week before it starts.
 g in case they made the situation worse.
 h so as not to walk in on a backlog the next morning.
 i so as to avoid any possible confrontation.
 j so (that) I need never get caught in the rain.
 k so (that) I remember to take them with me.
 l so (that) I would be hungry at lunchtime.
 m so (that) they wouldn't start worrying about you.
 n we will need input from everyone on this.

Use of English

6 For questions 1–6, think of one word only which can be used appropriately in all three sentences.

1 The company's offices are located on the ....*top*............ floor of the building.
............*top*............ managers don't always appreciate how junior employees feel.
The papers in the large envelope are ....*top*............ secret.

2 It was a long journey and I came to appreciate his ....*company*............ very much.
She's recently started working with a theatre .... in Tokyo.
You can't expect him to side with the employees – he's a .... man.

3 By all accounts, they ....*got*......*on*...... pretty good salaries for their age.
At school he was very slow at reading and writing, but he could ....*draw*............ brilliantly.
Such is the reputation he's built up, he never fails to ....*draw*............ a crowd.

4 He's very ....*to the*............ involved in the trade union and has been for a while.   *actively*
It's nice having a boss who ....*learn*............ encourages me to acquire new skills.
I decided to leave last year, but I've only started ....*to*............ looking for another post recently.

5 As announced to the press, the firm .... into several new markets last year.   +
Her laughter .... the tension in the room where people were waiting for interview.   *broi*
I have yet to speak to her myself, but apparently she .... her word.

6 Don't worry about next week – just concentrate on the .... in hand.
I know it's not my .... to tell you how to run your life, but I do think that you've made a mistake.
Despite his excellent track record, he was fired after falling asleep on the ....*job*............ .   *hsu too*

UNIT 16 Hidden nuances

Use of English

1 You are going to read two texts on creative writing. For questions 1–4, you need only give short answers. For question 5, write a summary according to the instructions.

Blue? Fearful? Terrible?

When writing a novel a writer should create living people; people not characters. A *character* is a caricature. If a writer can make people live there may be no great characters in his book, but it is possible that his book will remain as a
line 6 whole; as an entity; as a novel. If the people the writer is making talk of old masters; of music; of modern painting; of letters; or of science then they should talk of those subjects in the novel. If they do not talk of those subjects and the writer makes them talk of them he is a faker, and if he talks about them himself to show how much he knows then he is showing off. No matter how good a phrase or a simile he may have if he puts it in where it is not absolutely necessary and irreplaceable he is spoiling his work for egotism. For a writer to put his own intellectual musings, which he might sell for a low price as essays, into the mouths of artificially constructed characters which are more remunerative when issued as people in a novel is good economics, perhaps, but does not make literature. People in a novel, line 23 not skilfully constructed characters, must be projected from the writer's assimilated experience, from his knowledge, from his head, from his heart and from all there is of him. line 27 If he ever has luck as well as seriousness and gets them out entire they will have more than one dimension and they will last a long time.

1 Which word echoes *whole* in line 6? entity
2 Which point is the writer reinforcing in the penultimate sentence (lines 23–27)?

Hardly had

Grammar

If only for the sake of brevity and conciseness in a short story, the choice of the correct words in every phrase is of primary importance. Editors and their public are after the story and they want that story in as few words as possible, consistent with its being convincing. Those words, therefore, had better be the right ones.

In this connexion it is good practice to write a description of a man or a woman and then
line 10 see how much you can 'boil it down'. When you have arrived at one or two words which convey the full description, you will know that you have succeeded.

Let me urge the beginner not to use too many adjectives, and never to have a string of them following so closely in a context as to seem to be constituting a list. In poetry, adjectives are viewed with suspicion. The same may be said to apply to the short story. Never use adjectives unnecessarily. When a man is 'bad', do not tell us that he is a 'bad man'; tell us that he is a man and show him being bad.

Do not use the obvious adjective. Do not write 'blue' in front of 'skies'. Most of us have learnt by this time that the sky is not lavender. Avoid those adjectives which are commonly used in juxtaposition to certain nouns. 'Fearful temper', 'terrible tragedy', 'immaculate evening dress', etc. These adjectives, when allied to
line 30 these nouns, have come to mean nothing. Instead choose an adjective with real meaning. Instead of 'fearful' use 'unhealthy' or 'insane' or 'uncontrolled'. They mean so much more than 'fearful', since 'fearful temper' is a cliché.

3 What does the author mean by *boil it down* (line 10)?
4 Explain in your own words how adjectives *come to mean nothing* (line 30).
5 In a paragraph of between 50 and 70 words, summarise in your own words as far as possible the dos and don'ts given in both texts on word choice in creative writing.

the dos and don'ts

2 Delete the incorrect options in italics to make sentences that are grammatically correct and meaningful. Sometimes both options are correct.

a *Despite / Even though* she has a wonderful turn of phrase, she finds it impossible to write good fiction.
b *However / As* acclaimed the novel is, it is not always totally accessible.
c *Although / Whereas* he has written hundreds of poems, he has only had two anthologies published so far.
d *Despite / Much as* I enjoyed the autobiography, I thought it could have been shorter.
e Talented *as / though* he is, he has not yet managed to finish a single story.
f *As well as / As a result of* writing short stories, she also writes poetry.
g *Even though / However* powerful a phrase may be, it should never be used for its own sake.
h *As / Though* dramatic *as / though* her plots are, they are not terribly original.
i *Whereas / As* novels can range from around 150 to 1000 plus pages, short stories must conform to far stricter length constraints.
j *As well as / In spite of* several rejections, he has just had his first volume published.
k *Despite / In spite of* public expectations, the novel did not win the award.
l *In spite of / As a result of* their successful screenplay, they were approached by other film companies looking for scriptwriters.
m *As / Much as* I have already indicated, everyone thinks they can write fiction.
n *Although / As* adjectives certainly have their place in creative writing, they should never be overused.
o *Much as / However* I would love to be a writer, I know I don't have the self-discipline.
p *As / Whereas* I have hinted, poetry is not for me.

Vocabulary

3 Hidden in the box are 14 synonyms for *hidden*. To find them, you need to look horizontally, vertically and diagonally in the direction of the arrows. The first one is done for you. When you have found them, choose the most appropriate one to complete each sentence below. Use each word once and your dictionary to help you.

R	O	U	T	B	E	**S**	**C**	**R**	**E**	**E**	**N**	**E**	**D**
U	N	S	E	C	R	E	T	E	D	D	O	E	S
C	O	G	N	I	K	R	U	L	B	A	S	G	H
O	L	I	V	R	E	N	E	D	D	I	M	O	R
N	P	R	E	V	A	D	E	R	U	C	S	B	O
C	A	M	O	U	F	L	A	G	E	D	G	M	U
E	X	C	R	I	I	T	S	O	W	E	O	A	D
A	I	N	V	I	S	I	B	L	E	L	E	S	E
L	I	B	E	R	D	E	L	O	K	I	S	K	D
E	M	A	N	P	E	T	E	R	C	E	S	E	M
D	E	D	O	C	N	E	X	T	E	V	E	D	S

→ ← ↓ ↑ ↗

a It looked like a blank sheet of paper, but there was a message on it in .... ink.

b The .... lighting in the room was very effective and extremely tasteful.

c Many satellite broadcasts are .... so that they can only be received by people who have paid to see them.

d She was said to have .... millions of dollars in foreign bank accounts.

e Two new skyscrapers had sprung up and .... the view from her window.

f As I walked down the street I thought I saw someone .... in the shadows.

g Suddenly two .... gunmen burst into the shop and demanded all the cash in the till.

h .... by trees at the bottom of the garden, the factory could not be seen from the house.

i Her reason for confessing to a crime she never committed remains .... in mystery.

j The murdered soldier belonged to an army unit that specialises in .... operations.

k The troops had .... themselves so effectively that the enemy didn't notice them approaching.

l How dare you come in here issuing .... threats like that?

m Who sent you those flowers – have you got a .... admirer?

n In the book the author gives a thinly .... account of his own early teaching experiences.

4 Underline the silent letter in each of these words. Which letters of the alphabet are left?

answer	business
circuit	column
country	debt
gnome	handkerchief
indict	island
listen	marriage
receipt	rhyme
salmon	yeoman

5 Complete this poem with words from the box. You will need to think carefully about sound, spelling and meaning.

bead	bear	bird	both
broth	cart	choose	dead
dear	debt	dough	font
go	heard	meat	mother
rose	there	through	ward
word	work		

I take it you already know
Of tough and bough and cough and
    (1) ....
Others may stumble, but not you
On hiccough, thorough, bought and
    (2) ....
Well done! And now you wish, perhaps,
To learn of less familiar traps?

Beware of (3) .... , a dreadful
    word
That looks like beard and sounds like
    (4) ....
And (5) .... : it's said like bed,
    not (6) .... –
For goodness' sake don't call it 'deed'!
Watch out for (7) .... and
    great and threat.
(They rhyme with suite and straight and
    (8) ....)
A moth is not a moth in (9) .... ,
Nor (10) .... in bother,
    (11) .... in brother,
And here is not a match for
    (12) .... ,
Nor (13) .... and fear for
    (14) .... and pear,
And then there's dose and
    (15) .... and lose
Just look them up – and goose and
    (16) .... ,
And cork and (17) .... and
    card and (18) .... ,
And (19) .... and front and
    (20) .... and sword,
And do and (21) .... and
    thwart and (22) .... –
Come, come, I've hardly made a start!

A dreadful language? Man alive!
I'd mastered it when I was five.
And yet to write it, the more I tried,
I hadn't learned at fifty-five.

Use of English

6 Complete the second sentence so it has a similar meaning to the first sentence using the word given. Do not change the word given. You must use between three and eight words including the word given.

1 Despite her disappointment at his decision, Karen did not think badly of him.
bore
Although she ....
feelings over his decision.

2 The plan is unlikely to find favour with managers, unless the cost is greatly reduced.
probably
Without a great ....
reject the plan.

3 Whether I read for ten minutes or two hours, I rarely escape without a headache.
usually
No matter how ....
with a headache.

4 To appreciate the beauty of the lake you really need to be in a boat.
can
Only in a boat ....
the lake is.

5 I always end up crying in romantic comedies, however funny they are.
fail
However funny they are, romantic comedies ....
.... my eyes.

6 At night, our neighbours would always keep their cat in for fear it would get run over.
case
At night, our neighbours' cat used never ....
.... run over.

7 Having three children to look after every day had taken its toll on Elke.
grind
Elke was worn ....
looking after three children.

8 Profits have declined dramatically as a result of the recent downturn in sales.
led
The recent downturn in sales ....
.... profits.

Reading

1 For questions 1–18, read the three texts below and decide which answer (A, B, C or D) best fits each gap.

How you too can be happy

It will help you to be happy if you (1) .... in mind the following:

- Happiness is not a (2) .... to be achieved, but an emotion that is a by-product of what you do.
- (3) .... in terms of whether you deserve or don't deserve to be happy will stop you being happy.
- There is nothing wrong with feeling sad, which is the (4) .... emotion to feel after you have suffered a loss or disappointment.
- Depression is not just being very unhappy. We become depressed when we (5) .... ourselves for the disaster that has befallen us. Being depressed means feeling that you are utterly (6) .... , locked into some kind of horrible prison, where no comfort can reach you and you will not comfort yourself.

1	A have	B carry	C hold	D bear
2	A goal	B purpose	C design	D prospect
3	A Discussing	B Thinking	C Contemplating	D Envisaging
4	A suitable	B accurate	C appropriate	D valid
5	A blame	B disapprove	C accuse	D fault
6	A lonely	B alone	C apart	D individual

A rose-tinted view of childhood

How was your childhood? Did you like school? Was your little brother your mother's favourite? Were your parents too strict? Did you prefer books to sports? Here's a surprise. (7) .... matter what you think you remember feeling as a child, there is a good chance that you are wrong. In fact, a stranger taking a (8) .... guess would be just as likely to be right.

Such is the finding of Daniel Offer, a psychiatry professor at Northwestern University Medical School in Chicago. Dr Offer (9) .... 67 men he had interviewed in 1962, when they were all 14-year-old boys, as part of a study of 'typical' American teens. Thirty-four years later he asked the study (10) .... , now 48 years old, to think back to their teen years and answer the same questions. So many had changed their answers that, (11) .... , anybody taking a guess in the survey would have scored just as well. Dr Offer concludes that, as people get older, their (12) .... of the past changes.

7	A Little	B No	C Never	D Any
8	A controlled	B natural	C wild	D sweeping
9	A caught up	B turned up	C pinned down	D tracked down
10	A subjects	B topics	C objects	D patients
11	A statistically	B figuratively	C numerically	D collectively
12	A vision	B view	C outlook	D perspective

CHASING CHE

229 miles south of Buenos Aires, the twin cylinders of the motorcycle hesitated, then span into silence. The motorcycle coasted, ever slower, and came to (13) .... beside a ribbon of shimmery asphalt that stretched (14) .... across the horizon. The steel in the engine seethed in the quiet of noon on the Argentine pampas. I looked (15) .... , but there was little to see. The world, like my gas tank, was empty.

I had departed Buenos Aires early and left (16) .... its depressing outreaches within the hour. By mid-morning, the houses were gone, to be replaced by an absurd landscape, an abstraction of emptiness that welcomed utopian projections and offered a hallucination of perfectibility. No clouds, no buildings, no animals, no sound. And now no gasoline. It was not an (17) .... start to my first day in pursuit of Ernesto 'Che' Guevara, the 1960s icon of guerrilla warfare. Seven years before he and Fidel Castro shot their way into Havana and the history books, Guevara had passed this (18) .... , a young man in search of a future.

13	**A** stop	**B** halt	**C** pause	**D** rest
14	**A** non-stop	**B** continuous	**C** uninterrupted	**D** perpetual
15	**A** across	**B** out	**C** around	**D** over
16	**A** aside	**B** behind	**C** away	**D** back
17	**A** auspicious	**B** ostentatious	**C** opportune	**D** appropriate
18	**A** path	**B** route	**C** road	**D** way

Grammar

2 Using the words in brackets and adding any other words you need, turn these notes into sentences that are meaningful and correct.

> EXAMPLE: She / be poor and live in the country / be wealthy and live in a city. (far rather)
>
> *She would far rather be poor and live in the country than be wealthy and live in a city.*

a He could not have been / with your gift. (thrilled)

b Life in retirement / going to work every day. (good deal)

c There's / glamour in the film business / people like to make out. (not as)

d Country life / stimulating / city life. (nowhere)

e I / go out on the lake – I / good a swimmer / you are. (sooner not – nothing)

f We honestly feel / now / ever before. (fulfilled)

g By far / we ever / move to the country. (thing)

h She looks / young now / 10 years ago. (as)

i Performing on stage /scary / I thought it was going to be. (nothing)

j They / walk / go by car. (much sooner)

k Looking after a small house / work / looking after a large one. (not as)

l Everyone always thinks they / if they / money. (happier)

m All that good living is making them / ever! (fat)

Vocabulary

3 Complete these sentences with a noun from the box, using your dictionary to help you. Which are 'happy' and which 'unhappy'?

blues	boots	bump	crest
dumps	heart	moon	spring
tears	weight	whale	world

a We had an absolute .... of a time on holiday.

b There's been a definite .... in his step since he met Joanna.

c He's had the .... ever since his wife left him.

d The sun was shining and she was feeling on top of the ....

e He was over the .... with his new bike.

f She's been a bit down in the .... because she's got to resit her exams.

g Why do arguments with you always reduce me to .... ?

h She was carrying the .... of the world on her shoulders.

i Their hearts were in their .... when they realised they would have to tell him the bad news.

j Realising how little work he had done for his exams brought him down to earth with a ....

k After its election victory, the party was on the .... of a wave.

l His .... leapt when the phone went. Perhaps it would be her?

4 Choose the most appropriate synonym from the box for each adjective in italics in the sentences below. Use your dictionary to help you.

disheartened	downcast	hurt
melancholy	troubled	

a A funeral is a *sad* occasion.
b He was very *upset* that you didn't reply to his letters.
c Don't be too *despondent* – it's only a minor setback.
d You seemed a little *dejected* this morning. Had you had some bad news?
e She was rather *disturbed* by the news of possible redundancies.

5 Choose the most appropriate adjective from the box to complete each sentence below, using your dictionary to help you. Which two adjectives are left and what is different about them?

crestfallen	depressed	forlorn
glum	inconsolable	miserable
mournful	sorrowful	

a We heard the .... cry of a wolf.
b The forecast is for more .... weather at the weekend.
c Going to their rescue in a rowing boat is a bit of a .... hope.
d This is a severely .... economic area.
e They live in one .... little room.
f With a .... sigh, she folded the letter and put it away.

Use of English

6 For questions 1–15, read the text below and think of the word which best fits each space. Use only one word in each space. There is an example at the beginning (0).

Am I happy? (0) ....*Why*............ can't I be happy? Shouldn't I be (1) .... than I am? These are questions (2) .... nowadays plague us. In past centuries, people worried about dying and whether they would go to heaven, but (3) .... worries about heaven (4) .... more; we want to be happy now. Until therapists (5) .... along and told us to talk about (6) .... feelings, people rarely talked about being happy or unhappy. In most of the years (7) .... have been alive – I was born in 1930 – most people were unhappy and many depressed, but they kept their feelings to (8) .... Nowadays, (9) .... particular feature of the baby boomers and (10) .... younger is that they talk about happiness, and their lack of it, the (11) .... time.

We like to think that suffering ennobles us and gives us distinction, and (12) .... we like to think that previous generations had happier lives than we do. (13) .... Oliver James says, (14) .... *Britain on the Couch*, that in the 1950s people were happier than they are today, he is talking sentimental nonsense. The 50s were very tough and (15) .... many of us just plain horrible. I know, because I was there.

Use of English

1 You are going to read two texts on freedom. For questions
1–4, you need only give short answers. For question 5,
write a summary according to the instructions.

This morning, for the villagers of Chatharpur as for the inhabitants of all the villages around Delhi, distance no longer existed. Tributaries of an immense and triumphant stream, they flowed with the dawn towards the centre of their rejoicing capital to celebrate in its streets the end of a colonization most of them had not even known.

line 6

'Oh lovely dawn of freedom that breaks in gold and purple over an ancient capital,' proclaimed India's poet laureate in benediction over the crowds swarming into New Delhi. They came from all sides. There were caravans of tongas, their bells jingling gaily. There were bullocks, harnesses and hoofs painted with orange, green and white stripes, tugging wooden-wheeled platforms crowded with people. There were trucks overflowing with people, their roofs and flanks galleries of primitive paintings of snakes, eagles, falcons, sacred cows and cool mountain landscapes. People came on donkey, horse and bicycle, walking and running, country people with turbans of every shape and colour imaginable, their women in bright, festive saris, every bauble they owned glittering on their arms, from their ears, fingers and noses.

For a brief moment in that fraternal cohort, rank, religion and caste disappeared. Brahmins, Untouchables, Hindus, Sikhs, Moslems, Parsees, Anglo-Indians laughed, cheered, and occasionally wept with emotion. Ranjit Lal rented a tonga for four annas for himself, his wife and his seven children. All around him, Lal could hear other peasants excitedly explaining to their kith and kin why they were all going to Delhi. 'The British are going,' they cried. 'Nehru is going to raise a new flag. We are free!'

line 27

1 In what context is *tributaries* (line 6) normally used and why is it used here?
2 Explain in your own words why *they were all going to Delhi* (line 27).

'Good luck, Frenchman! From this moment you're free. *Adios!*'

The officer of the El Dorado penal settlement waved and turned his back.

And it was no harder than that to get rid of the chains I had been dragging behind me these thirteen years. I held Picolino by the arm and we took a few steps up the steep path from the river-bank, where the officer had left us, to the village of El Dorado.

Freedom? Yes, but where? At the far end of the world, way back in the plateaux of Venezuelan Guiana, in a little village deep in the most luxuriant virgin forest you can imagine. This was the south-east tip of Venezuela, close to the Brazilian frontier: an enormous sea of green broken only here and there by the waterfalls of the rivers and streams that ran through it – a green ocean with widely-scattered little communities with ways and customs worthy of biblical times, gathered round a chapel, where no priest even had to talk about love for all men and simplicity because that was the way they lived naturally, all the year round.

When we had climbed to the edge of the plateau where the village of El Dorado begins, we almost stopped; and then slowly, very slowly, we went on. I heard Picolino draw his breath, and like him I breathed in very deeply, drawing the air right down into the bottom of my lungs and letting it out gently, as though I were afraid of living these wonderful minutes too fast – these *first minutes of freedom.*

3 What image does the writer use when describing the south-east tip of Venezuela and why?

4 What is the significance of the writer 'breathing in very deeply' in the final paragraph?

5 In a paragraph of between 50 and 70 words, summarise in your own words as far as possible the responses to the different freedoms described in the texts.

Vocabulary

2 One word collocates with all the words in the box. Use your dictionary to help you work out what it is, then choose the most appropriate collocation to complete each sentence below. You may need to add a hyphen.

| fall | hand | interest | range | scot |
| set | spirit | standing | time | walk |

a He's been given a .... to negotiate with the kidnappers.

b She was able to .... after the charges against her were dropped.

c All political prisoners are to be .... under the terms of the amnesty.

d As my job isn't too demanding, I am able to do a lot of campaigning in my ....

e The accused got off .... because of lack of evidence.

3 Put these words in seven groups according to meaning. Then decide whether the words in italics in the sentences below are used correctly and, if not, which word(s) from the list would be more appropriate.

autocrat	cage	captive	cell
confinement	convict	custodian	despot
detention	elude	escape	evade
flee	free	guard	imprisonment
incarceration	jailbird	keeper	liberate
penitentiary	potentate	prisoner	release
reprieve	trap	tyrant	warder

EXAMPLE: autocrat, despot, potentate, tyrant

a Civil rights groups are demanding the release of the last political *captive*.
b The police have assured the public that the escapees will not *flee* recapture for long.
c He was sentenced to death but the president decided to *liberate* him at the last moment.
d Our mayoress sees herself as the *guard* of public morals.
e He claimed that his *detention* for anti-government activities was unlawful.
f When I was ill my room felt like a *penitentiary*.
g He was condemned for being a right-wing *autocrat* who ruled the country by brute force.

4 Complete these sentences with the correct preposition.

a Animals bred .... captivity would probably not survive .... the wild.
b She was sentenced .... six months .... prison.
c He's been released .... parole.
d Twelve prisoners are .... large following a series of escapes.
e Police are fearful a serial killer might be .... the loose in London.
f He's spent most of his life .... bars.
g She was stopped outside the shop and placed .... arrest.
h The terrorists once again slipped .... the police net.
i She was remanded .... bail until her trial.
j Police are holding the suspect .... custody.
k While she's away, I've got the run .... her house.
l After a month .... the run, the prisoners were finally recaptured by police.
m He's rather free .... his wife's money.
n My doctor told me I would never be completely free .... the disease.
o Not even his complete forgiveness freed her .... her feelings of guilt .... her infidelity.

Grammar

5 Complete these sentences using an appropriate modal construction with the verbs in brackets. There may be more than one correct answer.

EXAMPLE: All the hostages .... *must* .... *be released* .... (release) by midnight or the deal is off.

a Apparently, you .... (pay) by credit card here.
b For many jobs you .... (have) a good degree now.
c If it isn't too late, I .... (collect) that book tomorrow for you.
d Up to six books .... (borrow) at a time.
e I .... (phone) if I .... I just didn't get the chance.
f If you hadn't been so lucky, you .... (be injured) more seriously.
g If he had been doing his job properly, he really .... (review) the situation more than once a year.
h If he had entered the competition, he .... (win) a trip to New York.
i Survivors felt there .... (be) an investigation last year into the cause of the disaster.
j You .... (not stay) so late last night to finish the report. You could have done it this morning.
k It seems the number of human rights abuses in the country .... (fall).
l We were asking for trouble. We really .... (not agree) to go ahead without first finding out what the cost .... (be).
m The deadline was lunchtime and they .... (find) a solution by then.
n According to forensic evidence, he .... (not start) the fire.
o Judging by her behaviour, he .... (tell) her already.
p You .... (not drive) for hours without a break.
q I .... (not leave) my keys on the table if they're not there now.

Use of English

6   Read the text below and use the word given in capitals at the end of some of the lines to form a word that fits in the space in the same line. There is an example at the beginning (0).

Good *vibrations*

The woman twists and contorts her body, wheeling and spinning (0) ....*spectacularly*... across   SPECTACLE
the room, her voice rising in (1) .... whoops and yells then dropping to   ECSTASY
(2) .... moans and grunts before she collapses in a heap on the floor. And   MOURN
then it's my turn.

I came here seeking a brief escape from the stresses and strains of everyday modern
life. But right now my (3) .... stress flight response is in full throttle   INSTINCT
and urging me to sprint for the door, run like hell, anything rather than stand up and
perform (4) .... singing and dancing in front of a rather forbidding   SPONTANEITY
(5) .... of complete strangers.   SORT

But there is no (6) .... way out. And something about the trance-like beat   GRACE
of the African drums, the (7) .... hum of the harmonium, combined with   EARTH
the soothing candle-lit glow of the room and the serene (8) .... of our   ASSURE
teacher compels me to get up and twirl, stomp, groan and yell like the best of them.

This is natural voice therapy. The workshops are meant to release hidden emotions and
(9) .... and promote relaxation and mental healing through singing. Using   ANXIOUS
a mixture of mantra, Sanskrit chanting, Indian scales and pure (10) ....   IMPROVISE
coupled with movement and balance drawn from various cultures, the aim is to 'free the
inner voice'.

Reading

1 You are going to read an article about tapping into the unconscious. For questions 1–7, choose the answer (A, B, C or D) which you think fits best according to the text.

How to do hypnotic presentations

Hypnotism has a terrible reputation. We think it's all about sinister men on stage making people hop like rabbits or do stripteases. But hypnotism has far wider and subtler applications, and you can even use it to improve your presentations at work.

'We teach people to communicate with their audience's unconscious minds,' says David Shephard, chairman of The Performance Partnership, whose presenting course uses hypnotic techniques.

'We only use 5% of our brain power consciously, and the rest is unconscious. People respond, feel and make decisions with their unconscious mind, so any presentation will be much more effective if you communicate directly with that part of the brain,' he explains.

Alex McKie, a presenter who is studying hypnotherapy, adds: 'We get information at 2 million bits per second. The conscious mind can only remember about 32, whereas your unconscious takes in everything.'

Interestingly, the first step is to hypnotise yourself. Anyone who has ever given a presentation will be familiar with the racing heart, dry mouth and squeaky voice that nerves provoke. By hypnotising yourself into a light state of trance, you can overcome both physical and mental distractions.

Practitioners insist self-hypnotism is perfectly safe and claim that many of us spend much of the time in a trance-like state anyway. As David Shephard says: 'Watching TV is hypnotic, and so is driving a car.'

The technique involves making yourself comfortable, slowing down your breathing, then staring at a spot on the wall, concentrating on feeling relaxed. Gradually, start noticing instead

what is on the periphery of your vision. David Shephard explains: 'When you focus on one thing, the nervous system has a stress response, whereas peripheral vision makes you feel more relaxed.'

The technique has another benefit, too. If you use peripheral vision, you won't be distracted by the one person who is bored. Instead, you'll give attention to the whole audience and will be able to observe the overall response.

In the presentation itself, the principal hypnotic techniques involve your tone of voice, appealing to people's unconscious questions and preferences, and using stories and anecdotes.

'About 38% of your communication comes from the pitch, pace and tone of your voice,' says Alex McKie. 'So if you want to relax people, you drop your voice, talk much more slowly and leave lots of spaces.'

The next point is appealing to people's unconscious questions and preferences. 'People prefer to take in information in different ways,' says David Shephard. 'Some like to have information visually, some prefer to hear it, some want to experience it kinesthetically through touch, and others want logic. In any audience, people will have a preference for one of those four types of information.'

The trick is to use all four channels. So as well as talking, show slides or pictures, have questions or voting for the hands-on approach, and use a logical flow of information.

line 52

Unconsciously, different people in your audience will also be looking for answers to different questions. They are:

- Why is this information important?
- What are the facts?
- How does it work?
- What are the consequences?

According to David Shephard, by answering people's instinctive questions, 'your presentation will always be perfectly structured'.

Another powerful hypnotic technique is using stories and anecdotes. 'Storytelling is a fundamental way that we communicate,' says Alex McKie.

David Shephard adds: 'Metaphors, stories and anecdotes appeal to the unconscious mind and enable you to communicate a far deeper message. They make your presentation memorable and can have a huge impact on your audience.

line 76 'There's also the idea of "nesting" stories, where you start a number of stories but don't finish them. This keeps the audience's attention because at an unconscious level they're waiting for the end of the stories. So you have their full attention and they're captivated.'

The usual approach is to 'nest' stories at the start of your presentation, giving the main content, then finishing the stories to signal you're coming to a close.

Finally, you'll be reassured to know you can't get somebody to do something against their will using hypnosis.

'CIA research shows that hypnosis alone isn't enough to get people to do things line 92 against their wishes. It found it also required the use of psychoactive drugs, sleep deprivation or electric shock treatment,' says David Shephard, 'none of which is provided in our training.'

If you don't remember anything else ...

Remember that the audience wants you to do well. Hypnotic techniques help you and the audience relax so you can communicate your message more effectively.

1 According to David Shephard, why is it important for presenters to target the unconscious?
   A People are only conscious of 5% of their brain power.
   B People's thought processes and emotions are governed by the unconscious.
   C Communication happens through the unconscious.
   D The unconscious is the key to total information recall.

2 Self-hypnotism is primarily a question of
   A overcoming nerves.
   B slipping into a trance-like state.
   C feeling safe and comfortable.
   D being calm and relaxed.

3 Using peripheral vision is a technique which can help presenters to
   A let go of tension.
   B take in more detail.
   C deal with distractions.
   D be more alert.

4 How does the use of 'all four channels' (line 52) contribute to a successful presentation?
   A It helps keep the presentation varied and stimulating.
   B It takes account of the fact that people access information in different ways.
   C It takes account of the fact that an audience will prefer one channel to the other three.
   D It helps address the audience's unconscious questions.

5 What is the essence of 'nesting' (line 76)?
   A Using stories to communicate with the audience at an unconscious level.
   B Using stories to attract the audience's attention.
   C Using stories to hold the audience at an unconscious level.
   D Using stories to give structure to a presentation.

6 What does the second *it* in (line 92) refer to?
   A CIA
   B research
   C hypnosis
   D getting people to do things against their wishes

7 Which of the following best summarises David Shephard's view of hypnotism?
   A It doesn't deserve its bad reputation.
   B It is an underused medium of communication.
   C It can help people communicate more effectively.
   D It is harmless and cannot be subverted.

Vocabulary

2 Fill in the missing consonants to make eight synonyms for a phenomenon most people would prefer not to encounter, then use them to complete the sentences below, changing the form of the word to fit the context if necessary. You can use words more than once. Use your dictionary to help you.

c	g (× 2)	h (× 4)	l
k	m	n (× 2)	p (× 6)
r (× 4)	s (× 4)	t (× 6)	w

a _ _ a _ i _ i o _
_ _ o _ _ _
_ _ o u _
_ _ a _ _ o _
_ _ e _ _ _ e
_ _ i _ i _
_ _ o o _
_ _ a i _ _

a He is a man of great strength of .... and purpose, a man of great courage.
b People take such a .... delight in reading about horrific murders.
c The .... chocolate eater has been around – that box was almost full this morning!
d Our TV has given up the .... .We'll have to get a new one.
e Seeing the police car outside the house really .... them.
f The home team's .... playing ensured them a comfortable victory.
g He claimed to have seen strange .... at night.
h He watched the misty .... of moisture making patterns on the window pane.
i The awful .... of civil war hung over the country.
j His autobiography was written by a .... writer.
k Her .... rose as she read the letter.
l As a neuroscientist, he was particularly interested in .... limbs.

3 Complete these extracts with words from the box.

consciousness	hallucinations	images
instincts	intelligent	mind
panic	pathologically	primitive
psyche	rational	sense
unconscious	visions	

I have more than once been consulted by well-educated and (1) .... people who have had peculiar dreams, fantasies, or even (2) .... , which have shocked them deeply. They have assumed that no one who is in a sound state of (3) .... could suffer from such things, and that anyone who actually sees a vision must be (4) .... disturbed. A theologian once told me that visions were nothing more than morbid symptoms, and that, when Moses and other prophets heard 'voices' speaking to them, they were suffering from (5) .... You can imagine the (6) .... he felt when something of this kind 'spontaneously' happened to him. We are so accustomed to the apparently (7) .... nature of our world that we can scarcely imagine anything happening that cannot be explained by common (8) ....

(9) .... man was much more governed by his (10) .... than are his 'rational' modern descendants, who have learned to 'control' themselves. In this civilising process, we have increasingly divided our (11) .... from the deeper instinctive strata of the human (12) .... Fortunately, we have not lost these basic instinctive strata; they remain part of the (13) .... , even though they may express themselves only in the form of dream (14) ....

Grammar

4 Identify the incorrectly or inappropriately positioned adverbs/adverbial phrases in these sentences and reposition them. There may be more than one correct answer.

EXAMPLE: Unfortunately the witnesses by the time we got there already had in panic fled the building and there no longer was any sign of a ghost.

Unfortunately the witnesses had already fled the building in panic by the time we got there and there was no longer any sign of a ghost.

a Alone he sits all day long in his room, writing painstakingly up by hand his findings, on mostly scrap paper and usually in unfathomably long and complex sentences.

b The fortune-teller's predictions to my astonishment turned out to be accurate uncannily.

c Strangely enough, although it was dark practically, I was feeling actually relaxed quite as I patiently waited for a glimpse of the apparition, but that naturally dramatically changed when the room all of a sudden went cold.

d Never I've seen anything quite look so eerie or move so strangely – out of my wits I was terrified!

e There hadn't curiously been any further sightings in the castle of the ghost since last summer the previous owner left.

f The other day for the carnival he was very made up realistically – he just looked like the ghost of an old woman.

g Always he speaks on the subject of the paranormal intelligently, but the talk he later was giving generally was expected to be better even than usual.

h The computer for some reason started behaving rather oddly in the back office, flashing inexplicably up onto the screen strangely disturbing messages.

i The light mysteriously suddenly came on, although at the time no one was anywhere near the switch.

Use of English

5 For questions 1–6, think of one word only which can be used appropriately in all three sentences.

1 She was so upset when her grandmother died, she went to see a ....
Dance is becoming increasingly popular as a ....
I'm afraid they didn't have the gloves in a ....

2 Natasha could just make out two tall .... in the distance.
I don't know if we can afford it – we'll have to look at the ....
The .... and tables in that new reference book Simon bought are excellent.

3 It must be .... to live on the 43rd floor of a building.
He's got a whole drawer full of .... socks.
She does the .... teaching job to keep her hand in.

4 I don't .... having a dog in the house.
.... out – there's a stretcher coming through.
My sister has offered to .... the cat while we are away.

5 .... music originated in the United States.
Some unfortunate .... will have to tell him what's happened.
Although some people think her paintings lack .... , they are very popular.

6 When I looked in he was .... asleep.
He set the equipment up as .... as he could.
As far as we can tell, the protesters are standing ....

Use of English

1   You are going to read two texts on comedy. For questions
    1–4, you need only give short answers. For question 5,
    write a summary according to the instructions.

line 1   Comedy, it is often said, is the reverse side of the coin from
tragedy. This has become a commonly accepted truth, but what
exactly is meant by it? And how far is it true?

The main essential of comedy, of course, is that it is comic.
This does not mean that it must make us roar with laughter
constantly, though most comedies contain farcical elements
which do. The comedy of manners which came into its own in
the Restoration period (about 1660), works generally on an
essentially quieter and more restrained level than that of the
broad joke. The farce, on the other hand, relies on a good deal of
clowning, slapstick and ridiculous characterization for its effect.

Though the types of comedy differ widely, it is possible to
trace in all of them a shared assumption of what constitutes the
laughable. Comedy is nearly always concerned with the failure
of men and women to live up to the ideas they have of
themselves and of others. The writer of comedies works on the
assumption that human beings are fallible creatures, and that in
almost any situation they will fail to achieve what they mean to.

line 19   Take the classic comic situation of the man slipping on a
banana skin and landing in the mud: this is funny because there
is a sudden loss of dignity, brief proof that Man, for all his
knowledge, is subject to the same laws as the animal. Naturally
the more dignified or pompous the man the funnier his fall.

1   What does the writer mean by *the reverse side of the coin*
    (line 1)?
2   Use your own words to explain why a man slipping on a
    banana skin is *the classic comic situation* (line 19).

Comedy had its roots in a fertility ritual that
in ancient Greece was an occasion for crude
satire aimed at named persons. Already
during the lifetime of its supreme exponent,
Aristophanes, such personal abuse became
unacceptable, and an Athenian law of 414BC
forced the replacement of individuals by
fictional types as targets for attack. Aristotle
defined Comedy as written about persons of
minor importance whom their faults
rendered ridiculous. The 'New Comedy',
known to us through the Latin adaptations of
Plautus and Terence, had a restricted range
of characters: grumbling middle-aged men
and women, young lovers, boastful soldiers,
parasites, prostitutes, slaves. Superseded by
Mime under the Roman Empire, classical
comedy vanished from the stage during the
Middle Ages when a homespun variety of
farce was preferred, but was performed
again in Italy at the end of the 15th century
and soon gave rise to Italian imitations, of
which Machiavelli's *Mandragola* is the best-
known. The great comic playwrights of the
late 16th and 17th centuries, Shakespeare,
Lope de Vega, Jonson, Molière, drew on both
the classical tradition and medieval farce,
some adding a poetic dimension, others
making their plays vehicles of social criticism.
Writers in Restoration England and the 18th
century followed the pattern set by their
predecessors, widening the range of
characters and making use of sentiment and
realism. But after the Romantic period
serious comedy blended inextricably with the   line 3
realist drama that explored the problems of
everyday life. Only light comedy survived as a
distinct genre akin to farce.

3   How does the writer characterise early
    comedy in the first two sentences?
4   What does the author mean by *serious
    comedy* (line 35)?
5   In a paragraph of between 50 and 70
    words, summarise in your own words as
    far as possible the information on farce
    given in both texts.

Grammar

2   Complete these sentences using an appropriate form of *have* or *get* with an
    appropriate form of the verb in brackets. There may be more than one correct answer.

EXAMPLE: I won't be long. I'm just going to ....*get*...... my hair ....*cut*............. . (cut)

a Haven't you .... the sound system .... yet? (set up)

b When are you next .... the stage curtains .... ? (clean)

c She .... her unicycle .... last week. (steal)

d Can you .... someone .... the costumes to the studio for me?
   (deliver)

e I .... a very strange thing .... to me on my way home last night.
   (happen)

f He .... himself .... with a hilarious costume from the wardrobe
   department. (kit out)

g It's wonderful to .... people .... themselves in the old theatre
   again. (enjoy)

h She insisted on .... the theatre .... by a feng shui expert.
   (analyse)

i .... everyone .... outside the audition room till their name is
   called. (wait)

j The comedian soon .... us .... our heads off. (laugh)

k I won't .... you .... your weight around in here. (throw)

l I won't .... my auditorium .... a circus. (turn into)

m Why don't you .... Nicole .... to the party? (come)

n The administrator .... everybody .... application forms.
   (fill out)

o If you don't leave immediately, I'll .... you .... (arrest)

p Unfortunately we didn't .... the star of the show. (meet)

q He .... his foot .... in the curtains as they were closing. (catch)

r After you have .... the costumes .... , can you tidy up the props?
   (finish)

s Whatever you do, don't .... them .... jokes. (tell)

t Once we .... the lights .... , the studio warmed up really
   quickly. (work)

u I opened the door to find we .... mice ....
   in the wig collection. (nest)

Vocabulary

3 Which of the words in the box below …

a are synonyms for *amusing*?
b are synonyms for *smile*?
c are synonyms for *laugh*?
d are both verbs and nouns?
e are adjectives that can apply to people?
f involve making a sound?
g carry negative implications?

beam	cackle	chuckle
droll	facetious	giggle
grin	humorous	hysterical
jocular	roar	smirk
snigger	snort	titter

4 Complete these sentences using the correct form of *go* or *stop* with the prepositions in the box and an article if necessary. There may be more than one correct answer.

at (× 2)	by (× 2)	down	in for	into
of	off (× 2)	over (× 2)	to (× 2)	up (× 2)

EXAMPLE: I was passing your house, so I thought I'd
.............*stop by*............. for a coffee.

a She's really making .... her new career.
b I'm sorry, madam, but we have to ....
   the rules.
c The car slowed down and gradually came
   ....
d I'll .... at the shops on my way home and
   get some bread.
e I'd rather not .... that now. Can we
   discuss it later?
f There's a gas leak and the whole building could
   .... at any time.
g He's one of those people who will ....
   nothing to achieve his goals.
h I've .... the mouse hole with newspaper
   for now.
i Your speech would have .... better if you'd
   left out those appalling jokes.
j Have you ever thought of .... medicine?
k He used to smoke in bed when I first got to know him – I
   soon put .... that!
l Will you have .... opening this jar for me?
   I can't do it.
m The alarm should .... automatically as
   soon as smoke is detected.
n I've .... these lines time and again but I
   still keep forgetting them.
o They're .... in Malaysia for a couple of
   nights on the way to Australia.

5 Complete these tips with words from the box and underline the point of humour in each sentence, where the writer does not follow his or her own advice.

agree	always	apostrophe
avoid	clichés	commas
contractions	correctly	diminutive
double	end	exclamation
fragments	generalise	proofread
puns	specific	split
start	unnecessary	

EXAMPLE: Verbs <u>has</u> to ....*agree*.......... with their subjects.

a Prepositions are not words to .... sentences with.

b And don't .... a sentence with a conjunction.

c It is wrong to ever .... an infinitive.

d Avoid .... like the plague.

e Also, ... avoid annoying alliteration.

f Be more or less ....

g Parenthetical remarks (however relevant) are (usually) ....

h No sentence ....

i .... aren't necessary and shouldn't be used.

j One should never ....

k Don't use no .... negatives.

l .... ampersands & abbreviations, etc.

m Eliminate .... , that are, not necessary.

n Never use a big word when a .... one would suffice.

o Kill all .... marks!!!

p Use words .... , irregardless of how others use them.

q Use the .... in it's proper place and omit it when its not needed.

r .... are for children, not groan readers.

s .... carefully to see if you any words out.

Use of English

6 Complete the second sentence so it has a similar meaning to the first sentence using the word given. Do not change the word given. You must use between three and eight words including the word given.

1 He gets his audiences laughing uncontrollably with his funny jokes.
end
His jokes are .... hysterics.

2 Upset as she was, there was never any question of revenge.
last
Although ....
.... on her mind.

3 They pulled out all the stops for their daughter's wedding.
nothing
As far as their ....
.... much for them.

4 It is a good idea for parents to overlook their children's minor misdemeanours.
blind
As a parent, it helps if ....
.... your children's minor misdemeanours.

5 She hasn't stopped for a break in the five hours she's been here.
go
She's ....
.... five hours ago.

6 I wanted to tell her what I really felt, but in the end decided not to.
short
In the end, I ....
.... feelings.

7 Some youngsters broke into her car last week.
broken
She ....
.... last week.

8 I've tried everything, but he still doesn't deliver the punchline properly.
get
No matter ....
.... deliver the punchline properly.

Writing workout 1 | Letter

1 Complete this advice on writing a 'letter to the editor' by circling the best option in italics.

1 Open *clearly/vaguely* with a reason for writing.

2 End on a *soft/strong* note.

3 Try to *affect/engage* the reader.

4 *Develop/Review* the topic relevantly.

5 Include a good *balance/consistency* of comment and opinion.

6 Use *appropriate/formal* register and format.

7 *Avoid/Demonstrate* a wide range of vocabulary.

8 Use stylistic devices *effectively/liberally*.

9 *Avoid/Use* narrative or example to illustrate or reinforce points.

10 Order points *logically/progressively* and coherently.

11 Use *effective/minimal* paragraphing.

12 Make sure *organisation/grammar* and spelling are accurate.

2 Read this 'letter to the editor' of a popular science magazine and think about what is missing in the four numbered gaps. Then insert the sentences from below where you think they best fit, identifying the point(s) in exercise 1 which each sentence fulfils.

Dear Sir

(1) .... This surely cannot be the case for something that forms such a large part of our social interaction.

To make sense of laughter, we should look at it as a learning mechanism. What your article called 'cognitive' laughter is, I suggest, a way of exploring the boundaries of the rules for being a human.

In slapstick humour, we laugh as people fall over or get hit by custard pies. It is bad to fall over, because you might get injured. (2) .... This is a real lesson to a young child.

More complex jokes carry out the same process. The 'which side of a dog has the most hair?' is a test of the understanding of language. We laugh because the joke teller has deliberately misunderstood the normal way in which the words of the joke are understood. In a 'serious' situation, this deviation from normal language could be harmful. (3) ....

If language is an important development for humans, laughter at the misuse of language helps reinforce the rules for the use of language. This is all part of the play/learn process, but in a verbal context.

(4) ....

Yours sincerely

---

a Laughter, surely, is no luxury.

b And what about the clown who turns round while carrying a ladder over his shoulder, hitting his colleague on the back of the head?

c Your feature on the mechanisms of laughter suggests that humour is simply a luxury.

d You would not confuse 'side' meaning 'left/right' with 'inside/outside' in that job interview at a veterinary college.

3 How successful do you think the completed letter in exercise 2 is in terms of the advice given in exercise 1?

4 Look back at the text on page 14 (Unit 3 Reading), an extract from a magazine article on play behaviour among animals. If you wanted to respond by writing a 'letter to the editor', how might you order the following paragraph plan?

a establish a starting point for discussion through personal opinion

b introduce the subject of the letter / reason for writing

c extend the discussion in a new direction

d develop the discussion with reference to the article and personal experience

e conclude by questioning the implications for modern society

Optional writing task
Using the paragraph plan from exercise 4 (or your own, if you prefer), write a 300–350 word letter to the editor in response to the article on page 14, expressing your views on play and play behaviour.

5 Correct the grammar and spelling mistakes in this paragraph.

I tend thinking of play as spontanious behaviour what is having no clear-cut goal and no comforms with a stereotipical pattern and your article will seem to encourage such view. To me the purpos of play is simply play itself; it appears to be plesurable. But play also has benefitts: it is key of an indivijual's developpement, sosial relationships an status.

6 Complete this paragraph with linkers from the box.

as (× 2)	but also	furthermore
in my view	namely	not only	while

(1) .... a dog-owner, I know play is vital for proper development in dogs: games of keep away, chase and tug-of-war (2) .... develop physical abilities (3) .... help the animals attain social status by establishing superior mental and physical skills. (4) .... , play, (5) .... it often mimics aggression, (6) .... in the article, is one form of defence used to defuse potential confrontations. (7) .... , ritualised play in humans, (8) .... sports, serves an identical purpose.

7 Choose the best alternative in italics to complete this paragraph.

Recent/Up-to-date research *says/suggests* that play may be as important to life for us and other *animals/creations* as sleeping and dreaming. And no-one would *argue/dispute* that play is an important part of a *healthy/well*, happy childhood. But if play is necessary for the *active/physical* and *sociable/social* development of young animals, *including/namely* humans, what *happens/occurs* if young creatures are *hampered/prevented* from playing or *exploited/maltreated* with the result that their play is *abnormal/unusual*? Their *development/growth* may also be abnormal. *Certainly/Surely* the *behaviour/tricks* of 'problem dogs' *invariably/regularly* develops through *improper/indecent* games or lack of games when they were young.

8 Match the paragraphs in exercises 5–7 to an appropriate section of the paragraph plan in exercise 4 and order them accordingly. Then add an appropriate salutation, introduction and final paragraph to arrive at a complete 'letter to the editor'.

1 Which of these should a good review include? Tick the boxes which apply.

a mix of information and opinion ☐
b full details of what is being reviewed ☐
c name/title of what is being reviewed ☐
d mix of negative and positive points ☐
e relevant comparisons ☐
f examples to illustrate points ☐
g evaluation and recommendation ☐
h range of vocabulary, including specialist terms ☐
i variety of linkers and grammatical structures ☐
j personal anecdotes and hearsay ☐

2 Is either of these texts a review? Why? / Why not?

A

Born in 1930 in East London, Harold Pinter began to publish poetry in periodicals before he was twenty, then became a professional actor, working mainly in repertory. His first play, *The Room*, was performed in Bristol in 1957, followed in 1958 by a London production of *The Birthday Party*. Pinter's distinctive voice was soon recognized, and many critical and commercial successes followed, including *The Caretaker* (1960) and *No Man's Land* (1975).

Pinter's gift for portraying, by means of dialogue which realistically produces nuances of colloquial speech, the difficulties of communication and the many layers of meaning in language, pause, and silence, has created a style labelled by the popular imagination as 'Pinteresque', and his themes – nameless menace, erotic fantasy, obsession and jealousy, family hatreds and mental disturbance – are equally recognizable.

B

Harold Pinter's plays invite interpretation and reject it at the same time. You wouldn't be human if you didn't want to know what they mean, what is actually going on in them. But you soon learn that there can be no neat answers to such questions. The formula that will reveal all is beyond one's grasp.

No Man's Land, which has been revived at London's Lyttleton Theatre, is particularly tantalising in this respect. You never do learn the truth about the pasts of the two elderly men – one prosperous, one down-at-heel – who, attended by two possibly threatening subordinates, compulsively reminisce. They may be old friends; more probably, one has inveigled his way into the memories of the other, just as he has sidled into his house. What makes the impact is the galvanising self-descriptions. It's as if the dialogue has its own life – as if the characters become airborne on stories, talking their way into existence, out of the no man's land that is old age.

Optional writing task

With reference to exercise 2, and incorporating your own ideas, write a 300–350 word review of a well-known play or musical you have seen, focusing in particular on the interplay of themes and characterisation.

3 Choose the best alternative in italics to complete this review introduction.

Harold Pinter's *No Man's Land* is enough to give the reader a panic attack. The literary [1]*allusions/mentions* are so [2]*dense/thick*, the dislocation of [3]*character/personality* so [4]*mysterious/odd* that pinning down what's going on is [5]*impossible / like chasing a drop of water through a fountain*. But [6]*directed/managed* by the [7]*author/playwright*, this most [8]*abstract/metaphysical* of Pinter's plays is [9]*direct/immediate*, fully fleshed, [10]*filled/packed* with social detail.

4 Give the completed paragraph in exercise 3 more impact by inserting these phrases where they best fit. Use them in order and change the punctuation where necessary.

on the page
it's striking how little this matters in performance
at London's Lyttleton Theatre
it is also very funny

5 Match the adjectives (1–12) and nouns (a–l) to make 12 collocations which you can use to complete the paragraph below.

1	central	a	affinity
2	equal	b	characters
3	heavy	c	contrast
4	hidden	d	drinker
5	imposing	e	emptiness
6	inner	f	guest
7	literary	g	house
8	moral	h	justice
9	seeming	i	man
10	shabby	j	opposites
11	simple	k	paralysis
12	tragic	l	waste

The two .... are ....
They are bound together by a ....
Hirst is a successful .... He lives in
an .... in Hampstead. Hirst invites
Spooner home. Spooner is a seedy pub worker from
Chalk Farm. The spaciousness of Hirst's life, and the
achievements, represent everything that Spooner
has dreamed of. For Hirst, Spooner is what he might
have become. We are not dealing with a
.... between success and failure.
Hirst's success has turned to ashes. He is a
.... , essentially isolated (apart
from the presence of two dubious servants), living
in a state of .... Spooner only
outwardly embodies what he has escaped. The
.... is an emanation of the
well-dressed host's .... There is a
sense of .... in the play, of things
left undone and of unappeased ghosts. There is
some fine comedy. The new production does
.... to both aspects.

6 Use these structures and linkers, in the order given, to improve the style of the complete paragraph in exercise 5. You may need to delete some words and/or change the punctuation/word order.

who
-ing
whom
on the other hand
if things had gone wrong for him
not that
it is only (adverb) that
also
at the same time, it is the occasion for
and

7 Complete this paragraph in two different ways – one positive, one negative – by choosing an appropriate pair of words for each gap from the list below.

The leads are [1] .... Corin Redgrave as
Hirst and John Wood as Spooner both give
[2] .... performances. Wood is
[3] .... shambling and [4] ....
cunning, while Redgrave oscillates between
[5] .... superciliousness and
[6] .... flailing. Though Danny Dyer is
[7] .... as one manservant, Andy de la
Tour is both [8] .... and [9] ....
as the other.

a bleary-eyed/amateurish
b entertainingly/tediously
c flat/inspiring
d frosty/wooden
e ingratiating/uninteresting
f superlative/mediocre
g terrific/disappointing
h threatening/improbable
i unsettlingly/unconvincingly

8 Complete these sentences in your own words to arrive at an appropriate conclusion.

I must confess I find the temperature of the play
drops somewhat when .... To me .... ,
but .... a powerful and satisfying evening.

9 Combine your paragraphs from exercises 3–8, adding paragraph breaks as appropriate, to arrive at a complete review.

Writing workout 3 Essay

1 Choose the option (a or b) which you think best applies to an essay.

1 **a** factual   **b** discursive
2 **a** continuous prose **b** sections and subsections
3 **a** fiction   **b** non-fiction
4 **a** a specific topic **b** no specific topic
5 **a** informal   **b** neutral

2 If you were asked to write an essay entitled 'Space exploration: an investment in the future?', which of these points might you include and how might you order them?

a pioneering spirit
b unmanned rockets
c manned orbital missions
d the role of NASA
e moon landings
f the Hubble space telescope
g the solar system
h distant planets
i permanent space stations
j full-blown space colonies
k overpopulation
l The Milky Way
m the speed of light
n the universe, earth and our origins
o technological benefits
p space research
q live global television transmissions
r non-stick frying pans
s poverty, hunger, disease and war
t human suffering

> **Optional writing task**
> Drawing on the points in exercise 2 and your own ideas, write a 300–350 word essay entitled 'Space exploration: an investment in the future?' Make sure that your points are in a logical, coherent order, your style and tone are appropriate and your vocabulary is suitably varied.

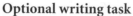

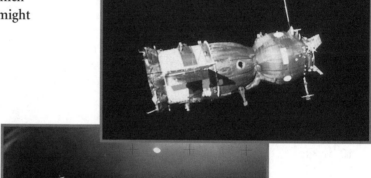

3 Read this essay. Which points from exercise 2 does it include?

Early unmanned rockets gave way first to manned orbital missions, then to moon landings and more recently to a manned space station, while probe-mounted cameras now buzz round the solar system, bringing more and more spectacular images of more and more distant planets directly into our living rooms.

These achievements speak for themselves and none of them would have been possible without the big inputs of time and money that have been made by the nations blazing a trail. How can you doubt, then, that space exploration has been an investment in the future – or that it still is, the prospect of permanent space stations just round the corner, let alone the more futuristic notion of full-blown space colonies for runaways from an overpopulated or messed-up world.

Don't you think the real question, however, is not whether space exploration is an investment in the future but whether the investment it represents is a good one in terms of what we get out of it. Some people reckon space exploration is

a must both for getting to grips with the universe, earth and our origins, and for its unforeseeable practical results in terms of technology and resources. Indeed the practical applications of technological know-how that is thrown up in the first instance through space research often pop up as examples of what's good about space exploration and you can't argue that, thanks to the space programmes, television pictures can now wing their way live around the world and non-stick frying pans can be used in the kitchen. But what's that got to do with the earth's starving millions?

Poverty, hunger, disease and war are bad news and if the nations that dominate the space scene devoted half as much money and effort to these problems as they do to space exploration much could be done to crack them. For the first time in history, the technological resources to combat human suffering really do exist, yet they are syphoned off for investment in a future that, for many, will never come.

4 Identify any words or phrases in the essay in exercise 3 which you feel are unduly informal and rewrite them so that they are more appropriate, checking your answers against the phrases in the list.

speed their way
significant investments
at the forefront of developments
There can, therefore, be no question
yet to be fulfilled
accommodating fugitives
environmentally devastated
Surely
represents
constitutes
worthwhile
return
There is a school of thought that sees space exploration as indispensable
increasing our understanding of
acquired
are regularly cited
the wider benefits of
certainly it is true
be transmitted
how has that relieved the suffering of
the world's greatest enemies
alleviate

5 Which of these sentences would you use to introduce the essay in exercise 3 if it was yours? Why?

a Space exploration isn't what it used to be.
b Space exploration has come a long way since its first tentative beginnings.
c To what extent is space exploration an investment in the future?

6 Write a short final paragraph to conclude the essay, then identify ways of shortening the essay to approximately 350 words.

1   Complete this paragraph so that it is true. First fill in all the gaps yourself, then compare what you have written with the words in the box below before finalising your answer.

A proposal is a (1) .... that is designed to be (2) .... It sets out – and (3) .... – a particular course of action in response to a particular situation or context. It is (4) .... in orientation and contains clear (5) .... Its purpose is to (6) .... , therefore both the (7) .... used and the ordering of (8) .... are persuasive throughout, reflecting the (9) .... behind the proposal. It starts with a (10) .... introduction, is appropriately (11) .... in tone and concludes with a suitably (12) .... ending.

convince	convictions	document
evaluated	formal/neutral	forward-looking
justifies	language	points
punchy	recommendations	succinct

2   Look back at the text on page 39 (Unit 9 Grammar) entitled *Put a little spirit into your work*. If you wanted to write a proposal based on the ideas there, how might you organise this paragraph plan?

a   Options
b   Conclusion
c   Benefits
d   Introduction
e   Looking ahead
f   Background

Optional writing task
A major international organisation is seeking ways to enhance its working environment for the future. Using the paragraph plan from exercise 2 (or your own, if you prefer) and drawing on your own ideas, as well as the information in the text on page 39, write a 300–350 word proposal.

3   Put these points in the most appropriate column of the table below.

a   yoga
b   the link between work and well-being
c   better relationships at work
d   t'ai chi
e   work more effectively
f   nice place to work
g   the importance of appealing to employees' hearts and souls
h   more profitable
i   greater staff retention rates
j   poetry seminars
k   increase in creativity and innovation
l   people need to be able to make a life, not just a living
m   improved morale and teamwork
n   workshops on philosophy, theatre or painting
o   an improvement of the interface between the organisation and its customer-base

Options	Benefits	Background
yoga		

4 Ignoring the square brackets, decide which column of the table in exercise 3 each of these paragraph openers (1–3) refers to. Then choose a continuation for each from A–C below and complete it with information from the table in 3.

   1 The value to employees of such measures is clear, but [research shows that] employers too can gain enormously.
   2 Spirituality in the workplace can take many forms. None are difficult to introduce and [, above all,] none are over-expensive.
   3 With 24-hour work-orientated culture the norm and stress at work common, [growing numbers of] people are looking for deeper meaning to life.

   A .... , ... , ... , ... and .... can all help to ease stress and get a better balance between work and home.
   B Organisational psychologists specialising in .... [cannot] highlight [strongly enough] .... as well as their minds and pockets: ....
   C Understanding the part the spiritual side can play in our lives helps build .... and thus enables people to .... [Furthermore,] a spiritually-friendly workplace is [more than just] a .... It can also be .... , with .... , hence lower recruitment costs, and it can see an .... , ... , and an ....

5 Make the three paragraphs in exercise 4 more persuasive by substituting these words and expressions where you think they best fit.

alleviate	beyond dispute
cost-prohibitive	dimension
healthier	promote
role	searching
serve	stand to
stress (v)	widespread

6 Which of the words and phrases in brackets in exercise 4 could be omitted? What effect would this have?

7 Give the following paragraph more impact by inserting the words and phrases below where they best fit. Use them in order and change the punctuation where necessary.

> Experts predict that understanding the spiritual will become part of workplace human development. It will feature in management training and will have a place in every organisation.

such an important (...) that
begin to regularly
eventually
in some form or another
no matter how small

8 Improve the style of this paragraph by substituting the phrases from the list below where they best fit. They are not in order.

> Introducing spirituality to this workplace now would make everyone happy, be good now for all involved and be good over time with a more productive workforce and increased profitability. At the same time, the possible effect on the organisation's internal and external relations would be big; so would the use of being involved in such developments.

offer long-term rewards
should not be underestimated
as well as
at the forefront of the workplace spiritual revolution
in the guise of
not only be unanimously welcomed
neither should the PR value to the organisation
it would also reap immediate benefits
the potential impact

9 Match the paragraphs in exercises 4–8 to an appropriate section of the paragraph plan in exercise 2 and order them accordingly. Then write an appropriate introduction to arrive at a complete proposal.

Writing workout 5 Article

1 In any article, which of these are important for holding a reader's attention and which are important for attracting it in the first place? Write H (holding), A (attracting) or B (both).

1 appropriate style and tone ☐
2 appropriate register for target readers ☐
3 a variety of grammatical structures and stylistic devices ☐
4 a good range of vocabulary and expressions ☐
5 a catchy title ☐
6 an interesting angle ☐
7 an intriguing opening paragraph ☐
8 clear development of subject/topic ☐
9 a strong final message ☐
10 a logical structure and smooth flow ☐

2 Compare the two photos below and choose a word from each pair to describe each one.

1 adventure/commuting
2 convenience/power
3 glamour/reliability
4 economy/performance
5 practicality/thrills
6 comfort/style

3 Complete this paragraph with words from the box.

aerodynamic	commuter
control	cruiser
handling	machines
motorcycle	spacious

A magnificent combination of sleek (1) .... styling, smooth comfortable (2) .... and (3) .... carrying capacity. The luxurious Honda Foresight delivers (4) .... performance with confident (5) .... at all times, making it an effective (6) .... as well as an excellent (7) .... Features include Honda's Dual Combined Braking system, used on some of our larger (8) ....

Optional writing task
The college magazine editor has invited contributions to a special feature entitled 'Getting around: motorbike or scooter?' With reference to exercises 1–3 and incorporating your own ideas, write a 300–350 word article for the feature.

Honda CBR 900RR Fireblade, icon of modern motorcycling

Honda's FES250 Foresight, possibly the safest scooter on the road

4 Compare these three paragraphs as possible openers for the article in the writing task on page 92. Which do you think is most appropriate and why? Think about angle, style and tone.

a People who ride powerful motorcycles tend to look down on scooters because they don't conform to their lifestyle image. However scooters are actually the fastest growing sector of the two-wheeled market and offer a great deal more than the economy and convenience for which they have a reputation.

b Mention motorbikes and most people think of speed, excitement, glamour, adventure and the freedom of the open road. Mention scooters, on the other hand, and more mundane considerations like economy, comfort, convenience, practicality and reliability probably come to mind. Yet scooters are currently the fastest growing sector of the two-wheeled market. Are they really all bought by sad individuals who can't hack a real bike? If that's what you think, read on and prepare to be surprised.

c Scooters are so cool. I've had mine for three weeks now and love it to bits. I couldn't imagine life without it. It's blue and I call it 'Scoot'. It's got so much going for it – it's cheap to run, ever so convenient, incredibly easy to ride and wonderfully trendy. Everybody wants a scooter these days – have you noticed how many more there are on the road? I don't know much about motorcycles, but what do I need to know? As far as I'm concerned, scooters are where it's at.

5 Complete this paragraph with words from the box. Which paragraph in exercise 4 is it closest to in style?

all	already	along with	but
just	to date	still	when

At (1) .... over 15 months old, the machine I own has clocked up 50,000 km (2) .... and is (3) .... running. It was purchased for travel, not for showing off or racing between motorway stops, (4) .... for covering ground economically, conveniently and comfortably. (5) .... , we have covered 34 different countries on various trips, (6) .... the more usual transportation at home – (7) .... on incredibly low fuel consumption, sustaining 120 kph (8) .... not off the road.

6 Find words in the paragraph in exercise 5 which you can replace with these more colourful collocations to make the paragraph more interesting.

a adventure expeditions
b beaten track
c convenient commuting
d going strong
e long distances
f motorway speeds
g service areas
h two-wheeler

7 Choosing a word from each column, make three collocations to complete the paragraph below. Then rewrite the opening sentence as a rhetorical question that links appropriately to the paragraph in exercise 5.

large	windcheating	compartment
secure	comfortable	bodywork
stylish	luggage	seat

The source of such a wonderful mix of convenience, economy and adventure is a Honda, but not a Fireblade – a Foresight. Yes, 250cc of value for money and dependability, packaged in .... , with a .... and a .... It won't pull wheelies, but it will hold a steady 120 kph and comfortably cover 700+ kilometres without refuelling.

8 Which of these points might you consider including in the final paragraph of the article? Tick the boxes that apply and write a final paragraph.

☐ a list of places the writer has travelled to and what he found there
☐ an evaluation of the Foresight's performance against the writer's purchase criteria
☐ a description of how well the Foresight has worn
☐ details of any concerns the writer might have

9 Choose a title for the article from the list.

a Travelling with Foresight …
b My two-wheeler and I
c Why I like my scooter

Writing workout 6 Report

1 Match the two halves of these guidelines.

How to write a good report

1 Start with a clear picture
2 Keep the target reader in mind at all times
3 Draw up a detailed content plan
4 Start with a brief introduction
5 Use effective paragraphing and other organising devices
6 Use an impersonal style
7 Use a good range of relevant vocabulary
8 Be succinct
9 Use a level of formality

a and aim to inform.
b and a variety of grammatical structures.
c and keep to the point.
d and neutral tone throughout.
e of the scope and purpose of the report.
f organised around a clear structure.
g that is appropriate to the target reader.
h that links with the title.
i such as bullets and signposting, as appropriate.

2 Look at this extract from a course brochure. Who is the course for and what is DTP?

Good Design using DTP

Duration: 2 days
Venue: The Training Centre, Regent Street, London
Tutor: Will Render

They gave you a desktop-publishing system and now they expect you to design ads, brochures, leaflets and reports, but you're not a trained designer. Don't worry – practical help is at hand! After this comprehensive and highly enjoyable two-day course you'll be producing work to be proud of.

Programme:
Design considerations with DTP   *What software to use*
Typography and fonts   *Font size and style*
Layout and balance   *Designing on-screen*
Graphics and logos   *Looking for the original angle*
Colour considerations   *Making the most of colour*
Proofing and printing   *Colour proofs / film output*
Practical exercises   *Hands-on experience*

Optional writing task

Imagine you were sent on *Good Design using DTP* by the company you work for. With reference to exercises 1 and 2 and incorporating your own ideas, write a 300–350 word report on the course for your boss. Make up any information you need.

3   What do you think of this as an introduction to a report? How would you change it to make it more suitable?

> My reason for writing is because I attended the course *Good Design using DTP*. Let me begin with general arrangements. I'll then go on to course content and finally I'll conclude with my evaluation and recommendation.

4   Without omitting any information, reduce this passage to about 120 words by deleting redundant words and phrases and by substituting more 'economical' words and structures where possible. Add any paragraph breaks you think are necessary.

> The *Good Design using DTP* course took place at the programmed venue of The Training Centre, an impressive building situated in the heart of London's Regent Street, on January 13–14. The facilities and back-up at The Training Centre premises could only be described as excellent. For a start, the computing room was large and spacious, a really good size, and it was also extremely well equipped and altogether very comfortable; each participant was assigned his or her own dedicated computer terminal to work on for the duration of the whole course, which was obviously ideal for getting a maximum of hands-on experience. The course was attended by a total of seven participants altogether. All seven participants had already had some experience of – but no training in – DTP. In essence this added up to a homogeneous group of beginners with compatible interests and abilities. The arrangements that were in place throughout the course were faultless and timings were consistently punctual. It was also heart-warming to find that there was a really good supply of refreshments on hand during the day and discover that considerable trouble had been taken with the lunches, which were very enjoyable. (195 words)

5   There are three errors of content in the following paragraph. Check back against the course details in exercise 2 to find and correct them, then rewrite the paragraph in a format that is clearer and uses fewer words.

> The three-day programme was quite intensive, covering a range of DTP functions and features. These were design software considerations with DTP, including what hardware to use, typography and fonts, in particular font size and style, layout and balance, with particular reference to designing on-screen, and graphics and logos, focusing on the need for an original angle. Colour considerations, proofing and printing were also covered. Throughout the course was highly theoretical, with ample exercises and opportunities for hands-on practice. Comprehensive notes were provided for reference and participants were also given a copy of their completed work on disk.

6   What do you think of the style and tone of these paragraphs? How would you change them to make them more suitable for a report?

> The chap who took the course was Will Render from Cambridge, a bit of an expert who teaches regularly at the centre. He obviously knows a thing or two about DTP and he's not a bad teacher either. He was pretty helpful, happy to bend things to suit us all as far as possible.
>
> All in all the course was great and I can honestly say I learned quite a lot about DTP. It also got my juices going and gave my confidence a bit of a boost, so that was really good. If you use DTP and haven't ever had any design or software training, what's my advice? Get yourself down to the The Training Centre and sign up for the course as quick as you can.

7   Combine the corrected paragraphs from exercises 3–6 and add appropriate subheadings to arrive at a complete report.

Answer key

Unit 1

Reading

1 c

2 1 **G** 'Our goal … high-flier.' (lines 46–47)
   2 **A** an ambitious … his wife. (lines 1–4)
   3 **H** Higgins … husbands. (lines 57–59)
   4 **A** she metamorphosed … events. (line 6)
   5 **D** "They meet … nervous?" (lines 25–29)
   6 **E** In company … code names. (lines 35–36)

3 **a** 'Don't look like a Christmas tree' (line 15)
   b ✗
   c restraint at the buffet table (lines 30–31)
   d restraint…on the dance floor (lines 30–31)
   e ✗
   f ✗
   g avoid conversations about … religion (lines 40–41)
   h do not interrupt if people are talking about business (lines 41–42)
   i never say how wonderful your spouse is in the corporate world (lines 42–43)
   j enjoy corporate events (line 44)
   k Know a little bit about the company (line 45)
   l show some interest (lines 45–46)

4 **a** block (line 3)   **f** boost (line 39)
   b coaching (line 13)   **g** high-flier (line 47)
   c modest (line 22)   **h** asset (line 63)
   d fee (line 24)   **i** obliging (line 66)
   e high-profile (line 34)

Vocabulary

5

A	C	E	F	I	G	U	R	T	R	A	N	S	D
C	O	N	V	E	R	T	R	E	T	C	O	E	X
B	R	E	T	L	A	L	T	A	R	R	V	V	Y
F	A	T	T	A	U	L	D	R	E	E	M	O	P
G	O	A	N	D	D	N	I	L	L	V	E	L	S
B	A	U	N	M	E	A	P	O	R	I	S	V	M
M	E	T	A	M	O	R	P	H	O	S	E	E	U
E	X	C	A	U	N	D	O	T	R	E	L	S	T
P	R	U	N	N	I	N	I	B	L	L	Y	G	A
G	A	L	L	U	M	R	O	F	S	N	A	R	T
Z	I	F	H	E	R	F	U	J	Y	W	A	S	E

a adapt   **e** mutated   **i** evolved
b altered   **f** transform   **j** fluctuate
c amended   **g** metamorphosed **k** revise
d modified   **h** converted   **l** developed

6 **a** scene   **d** ways   **g** places
   b hands   **e** mind   **h** clothes
   c baby   **f** bed   **i** subject
   a, **d**, **e**, **g**, and **i** have no corresponding illustration.

7 **a** made off with   **h** makes up for
   b get him down   **i** getting the message across
   c turn on   **j** carrying out
   d get these exams over with   **k** get the parcel off
   e turned out   **l** turned into
   f get the application form in   **m** turned down
   g gets around

Grammar

8 1 have found   4 have been   7 was happening
   2 was burning   5 have been   8 was being done
   3 had been   6 was   9 was experiencing

   10 passed   18 were
   11 settled   19 seemed
   12 realised   20 had just been handed
   13 (had) meant   21 grew
   14 tried   22 grew
   15 was / had been described 23 had come
   16 was / had been   24 have gone
   17 looked

Unit 2

Summary skills

1 **b**
2 **c**
3 Points **c** and **h** are not included in the text.
4 **a** Camels cannot be recommended for covering distances quickly, for conducting scientific fieldwork or for conveying fragile cargoes.
   b Camels are second to none, however, for gaining access to the desert proper, for becoming one with it and for experiencing its emptiness, space and silence.

Grammar

5 1 'm not going to be / won't be
   2 's heading
   3 leaves
   4 's going to be / 'll be
   5 'll be helping / 'm going to be helping
   6 's opening
   7 're / were on the brink of
   8 manages
   9 'll be
   10 will (be)

11 shall
12 'm going to visit / 'm visiting
13 'm / 'll be
14 gets
15 won't be / isn't going to be
16 'll be celebrating / 's celebrating
17 's / 's going to be / 'll be
18 'll check
19 are showing
20 like
21 'll give me
22 'm packing

23 will be developing
24 will have acquired
25 will also be considered
26 will be / are
27 will also be expected
28 will be
29 will

30 will move
31 are likely to
32 may/could have
33 will remain
34 breaks
35 will remain

Vocabulary

6   a eyed
    b mouthing
    c elbowed
    d shoulder
    e arming
    f thumbed
    g ribbed
    h heads
    i face
    j voiced

7   a had no doubt
    b had no problem following
    c had no desire
    d had no qualms
    e have no chance of finishing
    f had no option but
    g had no appeal

Use of English

8   1 apprehension
    2 outnumbering
    3 disquiet
    4 understandable
    5 unwieldy
    6 illogical
    7 powerless
    8 expertise
    9 manageable
    10 sleeplessness

9   1 one
    2 up
    3 from
    4 who
    5 of
    6 into
    7 before
    8 For
    9 every/each
    10 Now
    11 that/which
    12 at
    13 itself
    14 own/heated
    15 will

Unit 3

Reading

1   1 C   2 A   3 D   4 C   5 B   6 D   7 B   8 A

Grammar

2   a wouldn't shelter → don't shelter
       Unless male deer shelter in bad weather, it could be a
       matter of life and death for them.
    b has become → becomes
       Provided Bright Light therapy becomes more widely
       available, the number of winter blues sufferers will/could fall.
    c would happen → (should) happen
       Should you happen to notice anything strange, kindly
       make a note of it for me.

    d had → would have
       If jetlag were a figment of the imagination, air travellers
       would have no problems on arrival at their destination.
    e should cause → can cause
       Given that the sun can cause permanent damage to your
       eyes, you shouldn't look directly at it.
    f would be heading → will be heading
       If we don't pay more attention to environmental issues, this
       planet will be heading for destruction.
    g would be able → will be able
       If you stay calm, we will be able to assess the situation
       quickly.
    h hadn't ever survived → would never have survived
       Without luck on our side, we would never have survived
       the storm and returned safe and sound.
    i is → will be
       As long as there is a red sky at night, it will be fine the next
       day.
    j must → may/might
       Provided you don't spend long periods of time above 5500
       metres, you shouldn't experience the ill effects of altitude.
    k didn't persevere → hadn't persevered
       But for your perseverance with your research, / But for the
       fact that you persevered with your research, you would
       have no evidence to support your theory now.
    l took → take
       As long as you take time to acclimatise when you arrive in a
       hot country, you won't be asking for trouble.
    m haven't worn → don't wear
       On condition that you don't wear those ridiculous trousers,
       I'll agree to come to the party.

Vocabulary

3   a ways
    b actions
    c conduct
    d bearing
    e deportment
    f demeanour
    g habits

4   a affect → effect
    b loose → lose
    c raise → rise
    d practise → practice
    e descendants → ancestors
    f industrious → industrial
    g alternate → alternative
    h Beside → Besides; experiences → experience

5   a sure sign
    b strong hunch
    c strange foreboding
    d second sight
    e funny feeling
    f sneaking suspicion
    g bad omen
    h Sixth sense
    i female intuition

Unit 4
Summary skills

1 c

2

Attributes of good feta
very white
moist
fresh, slightly sour, pleasantly salty taste
woody flavour
not too salty, not too sweet

Factors influencing the flavour of feta
whether or not it is matured in tins or in wooden barrels
the salting process – amount and timing
the food eaten by the sheep producing the milk for the cheese – whether they graze and/or eat commercial food
what plants the sheep graze on
what time of year they graze (seasonal plants)
slight variations in the manufacturing process

3 Although <u>simple in theory</u>, the <u>production of feta needs extremely skilled cheese-makers</u>. The <u>secret of feta is in the salting</u> of the curds, which happens twice – <u>half an hour after they are placed in the moulds and again an hour later</u>. <u>This procedure prevents the development of the micro-organisms that would have made</u> a much sharper tasting cheese. The feta is then left to mature in either tins or wooden barrels.

4 Although not difficult in principle, the manufacture of feta requires great skill. The key to good feta lies in the way salt is added to the curds, which happens twice – 30 minutes and 90 minutes after they have been poured into the moulds. This process prohibits the growth of bacteria which would make a much sharper tasting cheese. The feta is then left to mature in tins or wooden barrels.

Use of English

5 1 air 2 steady 3 nature 4 heavily 5 return 6 fair

Grammar

6 Where alternative answers are given, the first alternative is the one that is used in the original book. Note that over-use of *used to* is considered bad style.

1 informed
2 dates/dated back
3 wrote
4 was apparently observed / could apparently be observed
5 just appeared / would just appear / just used to appear
6 would be / was preceded
7 would all be sitting / were all sitting
8 had just caught
9 is
10 (would) suggest
11 is
12 all brought / would all bring / all used to bring
13 used to dangle / would dangle / dangled
14 rode
15 set
16 would assemble / used to assemble
17 was
18 was
19 would begin / used to begin
20 (had) opened up
21 always filled / would always fill / always used to fill
22 could
23 might/would bring / might/would have brought

Vocabulary

7 **Flavour:** aromatic, bland, delectable, insipid, palatable, salty, savoury, tasteless, tasty, unappetising, woody
Texture: clotted, creamy, grainy, hard, light, moist, mushy, set, smooth

8 a quenching f fat   k dried
   b watering   g baked   l centred
   c food   h style   m bodied
   d range   i fried   n cooked/made
   e butter   j thin

9 1 masters   5 vegetables   9 natural
   2 cultures   6 chef   10 sharpening
   3 fresh   7 different
   4 poach   8 quality

Use of English

10 1 are thought to have been introduced
   2 put his success down to
   3 has the highest per capita consumption of cheese
   4 could have failed to notice
   5 went as/so far as to divulge
   6 application for leave was turned down
   7 to get a job unless you have (some)
   8 were nothing if not / could not have been more

Unit 5
Reading

1	1 C	2 B	3 D	4 C	5 D	6 B
	7 A	8 B	9 A	10 C	11 D	12 A
	13 A	14 D	15 B	16 A	17 D	18 C

Grammar

2

Noun	Countable	Uncountable	Noun	Countable	Uncountable
advice	X	✓	machinery	X	✓
appliance	✓	X	money	X	✓
business	✓	✓	parking	X	✓
cash	X	✓	preference	✓	✓
clothing	X	✓	produce	X	✓
competition	✓	✓	product	✓	X
complaint	✓	✓	promotion	✓	✓
equipment	X	✓	publicity	X	✓
experience	✓	✓	right	✓	✓
furniture	X	✓	shopping	X	✓
information	X	✓	success	✓	✓

3 a some/the furniture
   b appliances
   c a complaint / (some) complaints
   d successes
   e a promotion
   f parking
   g a preference / any preference(s)
   h (some) money
   i The publicity
   j cash / any cash
   k business
   l (Some) businesses
   m a competition / competitions
   n Competition

4 The following are correct:
   a are   e has/have   i is   m is/are
   b are   f are   j are   n has
   c votes/vote   g is/are   k were
   d is   h has/have   l is/are

Vocabulary

5 1 *complaints:* credit note, defect, faulty goods, legal rights, malpractice, money back, returns
   2 *aspirations/values:* affluence, image, lifestyle, possessions, status
   3 *sales outlets:* department store, Internet, mail order, supermarket, superstore
   4 *people:* consumers, customers, designers, retailers, sales assistants, shoppers, shopaholics

6 a consumer   c advertising   e retail
   b shopping   d market

7 a be in the *right/wrong*
   b be the *right/wrong* way round
   c be within your *rights*
   d catch somebody on the *wrong* foot
   e do the *right/wrong* thing
   f get hold of the *wrong* end of the stick
   g get on the *right/wrong* side of
   h get out of bed on the *wrong* side
   i rub somebody up the *wrong* way
   j strike the *right/wrong* note
   k start off on the *right/wrong* foot
   l the *rights* and *wrongs* of something
   m two *wrongs* don't make a *right*

8 a got on the right side of
   b the rights and wrongs of
   c started off on the wrong foot
   d barking up the wrong tree
   e the right/wrong way round
   f rub each other up the wrong way
   g do the right thing

Use of English

9 1 pursuits   6 consumer
   2 medical   7 attractive
   3 overtaking   8 fistfuls
   4 heavily   9 anxiety
   5 homelessness   10 unemotional

Unit 6

Summary writing

1 1 a B b A   2 a A b B   3 a A b B

2 1 A: this is exactly what a concert should be – risky and revelatory (lines 11–12)
   2 B: the fingers of his left hand crawled like a powerful and menacing spider up and down the mandolin. She saw the tendons moving and rippling beneath the skin, and then she saw that a symphony of expressions was passing over his face; at times serene, at times suddenly furious, occasionally smiling, from time to time stern and dictatorial, and then coaxing and gentle. (lines 16–24)
   3 A: For those who believe a conductor should be in absolute control of each note from every player all of the time, this could have been a frustrating experience. But for those who see music as a responsible and responsive partnership between orchestra and director, it was heaven. (lines 16–22)
   4 B: It made her want to dance or do something foolish. (lines 14–15); watched wonderingly (line 16); transfixed (line 24); she wanted to share the journey (line 31)

3 1 a (Text A lines 26–31)   4 a (Text A lines 24–26)
   2 b (Text B lines 26–29)   5 b (Text B lines 3–14)
   3 a (Text A lines 1–8)

4 *Suggested answer: 87 words*
   Essentially music comes down to notes, chords, rhythm and loudness, but in skilled hands those components have tremendous power. This can lie as much in the spaces between the sounds as it does in the sounds themselves. Careful attention to detail and the balancing of extremes contribute a certain excitement, with unexpected variations in pace and range adding drama, contrast and appeal. The real power of music, however, is its ability to transport the listener beyond the pleasure of the sound on an emotional and intellectual journey.

5 *Suggested answer: 70 words*
   Essentially music consists of four basic components, but in skilled hands these have tremendous power. This lies as much in the sounds themselves as in the spaces between them. Attention to detail and the balancing of extremes contribute a certain excitement, with unexpected variations adding drama and contrast. The real power of music, however, is its ability to transport the listener beyond the sounds on an emotional and intellectual journey.

Grammar

6 1 e   2 a   3 b   4 g   5 c
   6 i   7 f   8 d   9 h

7 a may/might/should score
   b may seem; can have
   c may/might not have given up
   d should have prepared
   e should go
   f could/can still learn
   g shouldn't have said
   h must be playing
   i can't both be learning / learn
   j could/might have passed
   k could/should have let
   l can't have been cancelled
   m can't have practised / have been practising
   n must have set
   o could/might/may have forgotten
   p may/might not have heard

Vocabulary

8 All the words and phrases collocate with *take*.

1 e 2 f 3 c 4 g
5 h 6 a 7 b 8 d

9

S	U	R	P	R	I	S	I	N	G	R
T	I	F	O	R	P	H	N	B	E	I
R	S	U	T	B	T	I	G	E	D	K
I	U	M	E	E	S	G	H	A	A	V
K	O	T	N	A	H	C	I	T	M	I
I	I	L	T	U	G	N	E	E	A	O
N	V	A	I	T	I	W	D	N	G	Z
G	B	R	A	Y	H	T	S	W	E	A
P	O	T	L	J	W	E	A	L	T	H

a strikingly beautiful
b potentially damaging
c obscenely wealthy
d highly profitable

Use of English

10 1 highly 3 cautiously 5 raise
2 drummed 4 brass 6 bow

Unit 7

Reading

1 1 F 2 B 3 H 4 A 5 G 6 C 7 E

Use of English

2
1 must be despatched today without
2 gone downhill since it changed
3 was young, I had no difficulty (in)
4 took any notice of her mother's constant
5 recent behaviour, it is doubtful whether/if Geoff will
6 their play (that) they were bound to win
7 you right if you fail
8 parents' consent to marry nothing stands in the

Grammar

3
1 produced   5 introduced
2 introduced   6 offering
3 introduced   7 Having been used / Used
4 considered

8 winning
9 playing
10 being cited / having been cited

11 using   15 coined
12 resorting   16 bent
13 Having studied 17 securing
14 going on

18 Having shown   21 lecturing
19 opening   22 teaching
20 specialising   23 being accepted

Vocabulary

4 eyes

5
a perceived   d behold   g imagined
b discern   e distinguish h envisage
c witnessed   f visualised i conceive

6
a back   e on   h through
b up   f into   i to
c forward to   g out for   j in
d up to (also *down on*)

Unit 8

Summary skills

1
1 (Black-backed) seagull
2 Wingspan
3 Up to 20 years
Text A: Seagull army invades inland towns
Text B: Bird-bites-dog shock as towns go gull crazy

2 Because they are no longer true sea birds.

3 Both texts refer to Alfred Hitchcock's horror film *The Birds* – to help create a visual image and to emphasise how frightening the birds can be.

4 1 h 2 g 3 c 4 a 5 d
6 i 7 f 8 e 9 j 10 b

5
a deserting (line 3)   h ornithologists (line 6)
b colonies (line 3)   i specimens (line 10)
c monitoring (line 11)   j opportunist (line 20)
d pest (line 21)   k species (line 22)
e dumps (line 23)   l paradise (line 26)
f flocks (line 3)   m scavengers (line 27)
g resorts (line 5)   n culled (line 32)

6 Text A: a, b, d, e, f, h, i, j, l, m, o, q, r, t, v
Text B: b, c, f, g, k, n, o, p, q, s, u

7 *Suggested answer*
Seagulls are leaving their traditional habitats and moving into towns, both coastal and inland, where they are thriving on the ready supply of food left on rubbish dumps and dropped in the streets by visitors and fast-food customers. Dramatic increases in urban numbers of these aggressive, sometimes oversized, birds have been parallelled by growing attacks on humans, domestic animals and other birds. Seagulls are particularly aggressive during their breeding season.

Use of English

8 1 that   6 by   11 than
2 They   7 who   12 far
3 do/achieve 8 from   13 made
4 them   9 around   14 of
5 As   10 Yet/But/However 15 with/serving/having

Grammar

9
a Scarcely had they joined the freeway when the traffic ground to a halt.
b Not until last month did the council start showing interest in the redevelopment scheme.
c Never before has the city received such imaginative proposals.
d Seldom is government investment in public transport remotely adequate.

e Hardly had the new transport network been open before/than a number of similar schemes were announced in cities around the country.

f Only once have I seen such deprivation and that was in slums that are now demolished.

g Rarely do/will town centre redevelopments achieve a harmonious balance between old and new.

h Only after the minister had finished his tour of inspection did he make his pronouncement.

10 a So stressful is life in some cities becoming that more and more people are seeking alternatives.

b Under no circumstances should residents take matters into their own hands.

c Little was the chairman aware that a petition signed by 50,000 people was about to land on his desk.

d Here once stood the sturdy fortifications of the town.

e On no account should you believe everything property developers will tell you.

f Not only was unemployment already a problem, but further job losses were also on the way.

g Such was the impact of crime in the area that residents were leaving if they could.

h In no way did they want to jeopardise the success of the scheme.

i Not one councillor accepted the invitation to view the development.

j Little did she expect the demolition work to start so quickly, and neither did I.

Vocabulary

11
1	development		5	divisive
2	built		6	favour
3	greenfield		7	problem
4	ill-planned		8	transit
9	populated		13	pressure
10	economy		14	reinvent
11	demand		15	prove
12	housing		16	architecturally
17	infrastructure		22	road-users
18	transport		23	Driving
19	job		24	hour
20	commuting		25	flow
21	air			

Unit 9

Reading

1	1 B	2 D	3 A	4 B	5 C	6 B
	7 D	8 A	9 B	10 A	11 C	12 D
	13 B	14 C	15 A	16 A	17 D	18 D

Use of English

2
1 has had a passion for puzzle-solving / solving puzzles since
2 objection to me/my taking the afternoon
3 was hailed as a complete success by
4 knowledge (that) smoking is prohibited/forbidden
5 did she know (that) her husband was about
6 must have misheard him
7 permits herself more than
8 does a contemporary work of art receive

Vocabulary

3 *Suggested negative characteristics*
Horse: ruthless, selfish, unfeeling
Goat: dissatisfied, insecure, irresponsible, pessimistic, undisciplined, unpunctual
Monkey: long-winded, unfaithful, untruthful, untrustworthy
Rooster: boastful, extravagant, mistrustful, pedantic, pompous, short-sighted
Dog: cynical, introverted, stubborn
Pig: gullible, materialistic, naïve, non-competitive

4 a Dog – noble, courageous, prosperous, devoted, selfless, introverted, stubborn
b Pig – naïve, gullible, materialistic, scrupulous, sincere, sociable, loyal
c Monkey – witty, enthusiastic, inventive, untrustworthy, untruthful
d Goat – sweet-natured, lovable, dissatisfied, insecure, irresponsible, pessimistic

5
a	un	c	dis	e	ig	g	in
b	dis	d	im	f	un	h	in

6
a	short	c	quick/short	e	peace
b	hard	d	sweet		

7 a semi b pre c out d self

What sign are you?
Rat:	15.2.72–2.2.73	2.2.84–19.2.85
Ox:	3.2.73–22.1.74	20.2.85–8.2.86
Tiger:	23.1.74–10.2.75	9.2.86–28.1.87
Rabbit:	11.2.75–30.1.76	29.1.87–16.2.88
Dragon:	31.1.76–17.2.77	17.2.88–5.2.89
Snake:	18.2.77–6.2.78	6.2.89–26.1.90
Horse:	7.2.78–27.1.79	27.1.90–14.2.91
Goat:	28.1.79–15.2.80	15.2.91–3.2.92
Monkey:	16.2.80–4.2.81	4.2.92–22.1.93
Rooster:	5.2.81–24.1.82	23.1.93–9.2.94
Dog:	6.2.70–26.1.71	25.1.82–12.2.83
Pig:	27.1.71–14.2.72	13.2.83–1.2.84

Grammar

8
a	ironing; putting/to put	i	to stay
b	taking; working	j	get; trying to clean; get
c	to improve	k	to be allowed to do;
d	being; being/to be		be made to do; to do
e	to defuse; avoid getting	l	to buy; to spend
f	to practise doing; using	m	lying
g	to embark; to suggest; to see/seeing	n	reading
h	meeting	o	to phone

9
1	to de-stress	5	to get	9	trying
2	taking	6	writing	10	to think
3	to bring	7	analysing	11	to enhance
4	to become	8	create/to create	12	to appeal

Unit 10

Summary skills

1 Text A: Globalisation – a positive force for all
Text B: A commitment to reduce inequality
Both texts appeared in a UK newspaper supplement entitled 'Globalisation', which was produced to coincide with the UK Government's publication of a White Paper on International Development called 'Making Globalisation Work for the

World's Poor'. Text A is an extract from an article written by the Secretary-General of the United Nations. Text B is an extract from an article written by the Permanent Secretary to the Department for International Development in the UK.

2
1	Essentially	10	On the contrary
2	partly	11	And
3	partly	12	And
4	Yet	13	And
5	Because	14	but
6	because	15	above all
7	because	16	But
8	Thus	17	Against that background
9	for	18	Or

3 **a, b, d** and **e** are seen by the writers as challenges facing a global world.

4 *Possible answer: 70 words*
Of primary importance is the maximisation of globalisation's economic benefits, *on the one hand*, and their fair and equal distribution among the world's people *on the other*. This will require *not only* new internationally agreed social values and policies, *but also* fresh approaches to government. *In addition*, the world must find ways to protect the environment and its resources, preserve peace, reduce poverty and disease, and extend education to all.

Use of English

5
1	language	3	globe	5	economic
2	rich	4	poverty	6	operate

Grammar

6
a spoke
b to enrol
c would try; would enjoy
d were
e didn't/wouldn't keep
f had had; would have been able
g would have passed; had worked
h was/were
i was/were
j hadn't agreed
k was
l sought
m to start
n had been done; had
o asked / had asked
p to have moved / to move; ran

Vocabulary

7
1	globalisation	6	nations	11	technological
2	beneficial	7	disempowers	12	transport
3	development	8	employment	13	integration
4	higher	9	poverty	14	harnessed
5	inequality	10	forces		

8
a to turn somebody down
b turnover
c turn-out
d to turn off a tap
e to turn in
f downturn
g turn-off
h to turn something out
i to overturn

9 a way b events c gave d good e every f twists

Unit 11
Reading

1 1 C 2 B 3 D 4 A 5 C 6 B 7 A

Grammar

2
a immensely/deeply
b deeply/~~absolutely~~; extremely/rather
c ~~utterly/entirely~~ extremely/fairly/highly/pretty/quite/rather/really/very
d woefully/~~fairly~~; grossly/~~absolutely~~
e absolutely/~~completely~~; extremely/pretty
f really/~~eminently~~; pretty/quite; entirely/~~quite~~
g rather/utterly; completely/quite
h ~~highly/woefully~~ extremely/fairly/pretty/quite/rather/really/very; quite/really
i ~~fairly~~/absolutely; utterly/~~immensely~~

Vocabulary

3
a (un)arguable, argumentative
b awesome, awful
c (in)defensible, defensive, defenceless
d fearsome, fearful, fearless
e (un)forgettable, forgetful
f (un)imaginable, imaginary, (un)imaginative
g momentary, momentous
h restive, restful, restless
i sensible, (in)sensitive, nonsensical, sensuous, senseless
j (un)usable, useful, useless

4
a	awesome	f	momentous
b	indefensible (also insensitive/senseless)	g	restive
c	fearsome	h	nonsensical
d	forgetful	i	useless
e	imaginary		

5
a	highly questionable	e	utterly banal
b	comparatively rare	f	radically reformed
c	heavily biased	g	ridiculously cheap
d	deceptively simple		

Use of English

6
1	round	4	down	7	end	10	what	13	stand
2	there	5	fall	8	which	11	One	14	ones
3	only	6	make	9	in	12	who	15	with

Unit 12
Summary skills

1
a Dr Russell Vreeland, a biologist at West Chester University, Pennsylvania
b inclusion, the trapping of liquid 'pockets' in crystalline structures
c *Bacillus marismortui*, the waters of the Dead Sea

2
1 the world's oldest surviving life forms
2 The previous record for longevity
3 A quarter of a billion years ago
4 inside the crystals of rock salt
5 using stringent sterilisation procedures
6 its suspended animation
7 removing the few microlitres of fluid from each inclusion
8 began testing their samples for life
9 modern cousin

3 **a** isolated   **d** dormant   **g** salinity
   b shaft   **e** contaminated
   c repository   **f** viable

4 *Possible answer: 70 words*
The Salado Formation – the name given to mineral and salt deposits in New Mexico which were created when a Permian-age inland sea dried up – has recently been discovered to be home to the world's oldest living organisms. The 250-million-year-old, previously unknown bacteria, dubbed *Bacillus permians* after their geological age, were found in the wall of a deep shaft leading to a subterranean cave at Carlsbad which now houses nuclear waste.

Grammar

5 **a** must be worn
   b must be extinguished
   c must be kept clear / are to be kept clear
   d may not be used / are not to be used
   e are allowed / are permitted
   f is reserved; will be removed

6 1 is dealt   6 is thought
   2 will be allowed / is allowed   7 have already been found
   3 are dealt   8 has been linked
   4 had been dealt   9 has been suspected
   5 are sprinkled

Vocabulary

7

A	Z	R	D	K	C	A	H
H	E	C	I	L	S	C	S
S	T	E	S	I	C	X	E
A	R	T	S	K	U	R	V
L	A	C	E	R	A	T	E
S	N	I	C	W	R	I	R
G	O	H	T	I	P	L	B
B	O	I	N	C	I	S	E
P	T	R	I	M	W	A	S

All 12 verbs mean *cut.*

8 **a** hack   **e** slashed   **i** sawing
   b slit   **f** slice   **j** severed
   c trimming   **g** incised   **k** excised
   d dissect   **h** chopped

9 **a** out   **e** back/down on   **i** up into
   b down to   **f** in   **j** down
   c off   **g** off   **k** across/through
   d across   **h** out   **l** through

Use of English

10 1 passionately   6 exemplified
    2 complexity   7 uncompromising
    3 labyrinthine   8 opacity
    4 expectations   9 incomprehensibility
    5 subtleties   10 uninitiated

Unit 13
Reading

1 1 D   2 C   3 A   4 D   5 C   6 B   7 B   8 A

Grammar

2 **a** Industry consultant William Moore acknowledged that recycling paper would never completely eliminate cutting down trees, but said it could mean cutting fewer trees.
   b Harold Barrington, a recycling enthusiast from Oklahoma, said that he had built a machine that made/makes petroleum out of old tyres. He claimed he had / to have produced as much as 1,800 gallons of crude oil in five hours. Apparently, he had distilled some into gasoline to run his machines and had sold the rest to a refinery.
   c Liz Newman, a mother of three, mused that we lived / were living in a world surrounded by concrete and she sometimes wondered what she could do about the environment. She concluded that she could sort her trash.
   d Recycling specialist David Dougherty questions why you would cut down a tree to make a newspaper with a lifetime use of just over 20 minutes, then bury it, when you can/could use it six times over, then burn what's left to create energy. He insisted we had to make recycling a natural part of the economy so that it would become a part of our lifestyle. He reckoned that, of all the environmental concerns that had come up through the years, this was the most personal. In his view, people were uncertain what they could do about saving whales or the rain forest. But they could recycle their waste every day of their lives.

Vocabulary

3 **Bad:** 1 i   3 e   5 h   6 c   7 d   8 a   10 b
   Good: 2 j   4 f   9 g

4 **a** support   **g** persecuted
   b abolished   **h** repair
   c discard   **i** indigenous
   d devastation   **j** refuse
   e money   **k** protect
   f environmentally-friendly

   1 d   2 f   3 c   4 b   5 k   6 i   7 h   8 j   9 g   10 e

Use of English

5 1 the   6 more   11 these/they
   2 but/though   7 for   12 which/that
   3 when/if   8 to   13 up
   4 into   9 not   14 Even
   5 of   10 our   15 us

Unit 14
Use of English

1 1 in a religious context – the writer is seeking to 'convert' people to oily fish
   2 the (small) risk to health of the chemical toxins known to be present in oily fish versus the (far greater) benefits to health of the nutritional value of oily fish
   3 they allow girls fewer opportunities than boys to go out and get exercise unsupervised because of concern for their daughters' safety
   4 also take the lift instead of the stairs

5 *Possible answer: 61 words*
As well as feeding their children a small amount of oily fish on a regular basis from an early age, parents should make sure their children get enough physical exercise. This is as important for girls as it is for boys. Parents should encourage their children to exercise by allowing them outside more and by acting as good role models themselves.

Grammar

2 a Research carried out by *the* Institute of Respiratory Medicine *at the* Royal Prince Alfred Hospital *in* Sydney, Australia, suggests that there is *a* correlation *between* the consumption *of* oily fish and *a/the* reduction *of* children's risk *of* developing asthma. New studies are also beginning to make *a* connection *between* a deficiency in omega 3 fatty acids and depression and mental illness.

b Jane Clarke is *a* state-registered dietician and (*the*) author *of* the *Bodyfoods* series of books. As *a* teenager she was interested *in* medicine but wanted to work *with* food instead *of* drugs, so she did *a* degree *in* dietetics *at* Leeds University.

c Everyone responds differently *to* food *in* the morning: some people feel sleepy and unable to function *after* eating *a* large breakfast, whereas others need *a* hearty breakfast before they embark on *the* day's activities.

d Chocolate causes your blood-sugar level *to* rise quickly, which stimulates *the* pancreas to produce insulin, *the* hormone that rapidly brings it *down*. Fresh fruits give *the* best slow-release energy boost so increase your fruit intake.

e Strenuous exercise results *in* the release *of* endorphines in *the* brain, giving athletes *a* natural 'high'. Some athletes become dependent *on the* effect, but it does not harm them *in* any way.

f Make sure that you drink plenty of water throughout *the* day to enable all *the* energising vitamins, minerals and slow-release sugars *in* the food that you eat to be absorbed *by* your body. Adults should aim *to* drink two to three litres of water *a* day.

g It is best to exercise every day. Three days *a* week is *the* absolute minimum. Work out *the* best time of (*the*) day to fit in *an* exercise programme. It is unwise to exercise if you are injured or if you have any form *of* fever or viral infection such as *a* cold or (*the*) flu.

Vocabulary

3 a avoiding
b trying
c asked
d ignored; left
e decided; ask
f take/persuade
g looked/searched
h enjoy
i beat
j continues; see
k promised
l advised/wanted/told/ encouraged

4 a get it off her chest
b up to my ears
c makes my hair stand on end
d head and shoulders above
e all fingers and thumbs
f pulling my leg
g keep you on your toes
h get my head round
i lift a finger to help

Use of English

5 1 inability
2 humiliation
3 endless
4 unwanted
5 achievement
6 unbelievable
7 statements
8 validate
9 disorientation
10 tiredness

Unit 15
Reading

1 1 G 2 C 3 B 4 E 5 H 6 A 7 F

Vocabulary

2 a bored – applies to a person, not a task
b drudgery – applies to (hard boring) work in general, not a specific job
c well-appointed – doesn't apply to a person
d remuneration – the only guaranteed/tangible benefit of a job
e indifferent – applies to a person's response to something, not the actual thing

3 a ursine
b feline
c bovine
d canine
e aquiline
f elephantine
g equine
h porcine

4 a elephantine
b equine
c feline
d bovine
e canine
f aquiline

Grammar

5 1 f   **2** i   **3** b   **4** e   **5** j   **6** l   **7** h
8 m   **9** n   **10** k   **11** a   **12** g   **13** d   **14** c

Use of English

6 1 top
2 company
3 draw
4 actively
5 broke
6 job

Unit 16
Use of English

1 1 entire (line 29)
2 the need for novelists to create living people not characters/caricatures
3 reduce the writer's description of a man/woman to its essence
4 adjectives which are frequently used to describe particular nouns gradually lose their effect through overuse and eventually add nothing to the meaning of the noun
5 *Possible answer: 63 words*
Words must never be used for their own sake or to indulge a writer's ego. Every word used in creative writing should be there because it makes a vital contribution to the finished product. With short stories, length is a factor so succinctness is important. In every genre, writers should use adjectives cautiously, selecting them deliberately for their impact and avoiding any superfluity.

Grammar

2 a Even though
b However
c Although
d Much as
e as/though
f As well as
g However
h As; as (OR: Dramatic though her plots are…)
i Whereas
j In spite of
k Despite/In spite of
l As a result of
m As
n Although
o Much as
p As

Vocabulary

3

R	O	U	T	B	E	S	C	R	E	E	N	E	D
U	N	S	E	C	R	E	T	E	D	D	O	E	S
C	O	G	N	I	K	R	U	L	B	A	S	G	H
O	L	I	V	R	E	N	E	D	D	I	M	O	R
N	P	R	E	V	A	D	E	R	U	C	S	B	O
C	A	M	O	U	F	L	A	G	E	D	G	M	U
E	X	C	R	I	T	S	O	W	E	O	A	D
A	I	N	V	I	S	I	B	L	E	L	E	S	E
L	I	B	E	R	D	E	L	O	K	I	S	K	D
E	M	A	N	P	E	T	E	R	C	E	S	E	M
D	E	D	O	C	N	E	X	T	E	V	E	D	S

a	invisible	**f**	lurking	**k**	camouflaged
b	concealed	**g**	masked	**l**	veiled
c	encoded	**h**	Screened	**m**	secret
d	secreted	**i**	shrouded	**n**	disguised
e	obscured	**j**	covert		

4 answer, business, circuit, column, country, debt, gnome, handkerchief, indict, island, listen, marriage, receipt, rhyme, salmon, yeoman
The letters which are left are: f j k m q r v x y z

5

1	dough	9	mother	17	work
2	through	10	both	18	ward
3	heard	11	broth	19	font
4	bird	12	there	20	word
5	dead	13	dear	21	go
6	bead	14	bear	22	cart
7	meat	15	rose		
8	debt	16	choose		

Use of English

6
1 was disappointed, Karen bore him no ill
2 reduction in (the) cost, managers will probably
3 long I read (for), I usually end up
4 can you really appreciate how beautiful
5 never fail to bring tears to
6 to be allowed out in case it got/was
7 down by the daily grind of
8 has led to a dramatic decline in

Unit 17
Reading

1	1	D	2	A	3	B	4	C	5	A	6	B
	7	B	8	C	9	D	10	A	11	A	12	B
	13	D	14	C	15	C	16	B	17	A	18	D

Grammar

2
a He could not have been more thrilled with your gift.
b Life in retirement is a good deal better/easier than going to work every day.
c There's not as much glamour in the film business as people like to make out.
d Country life is nowhere near as stimulating as city life.
e I would sooner not go out on the lake – I am nothing like as good a swimmer as you are.
f We honestly feel more fulfilled now than ever before.
g By far the best thing we ever did was (to) move to the country.
h She looks as young now as she did 10 years ago.
i Performing on stage was nothing like as scary as I thought it was going to be.
j They would much sooner walk than go by car.
k Looking after a small house is not as much work as looking after a large one.
l Everyone always thinks they would be happier if they had (more) money.
m All that good living is making them fatter than ever!

Vocabulary

3

a	whale (happy)	**g**	tears (unhappy)
b	spring (happy)	**h**	weight (unhappy)
c	blues (unhappy)	**i**	boots (unhappy)
d	world (happy)	**j**	bump (unhappy)
e	moon (happy)	**k**	crest (happy)
f	dumps (unhappy)	**l**	heart (happy)

4

a	melancholy	**d**	downcast
b	hurt	**e**	troubled
c	disheartened		

5

a	mournful	**d**	depressed
b	miserable	**e**	glum
c	forlorn	**f**	sorrowful

The two remaining adjectives, *crestfallen* and *inconsolable*, can only be used of people.

Use of English

6

1	happier	9	a
2	that/which	10	those (anyone/people)
3	nobody/no-one	11	whole
4	any	12	so/therefore
5	came	13	When
6	our	14	in
7	I	15	for (to)
8	themselves		

Unit 18
Use of English

1
1 in a geographical/environmental context to describe river systems – it is used here to intensify the image of people flooding into New Delhi
2 to witness the raising of India's flag of independence / to experience British withdrawal / the birth of the nation
3 land as water and water as land – to emphasise the density and extent of the forest
4 he is savouring his new freedom

5 *Possible answer: 68 words*
On India's independence from British rule, people from all over converged on New Delhi, dressed up to the nines and travelling by all manner of means; unified by the emotion of the occasion, they temporarily forgot all their differences. On release from imprisonment, the French convict first took stock of the remote surroundings, then savoured the start of his freedom with a conscious series of full deep breaths.

Vocabulary

2 The word is *free*.
   a free hand   c set free   e scot-free
   b walk free   d free time

3 elude, escape, evade, flee
  free, liberate, release, reprieve
  captive, convict, jailbird, prisoner
  custodian, guard, keeper, warder
  confinement, detention, imprisonment, incarceration
  cage, cell, penitentiary, trap
  autocrat, despot, potentate, tyrant
   a prisoner
   b evade (also *elude*; *escape* would also be correct but stylistically less appropriate)
   c reprieve (also *free, release*)
   d custodian (also *keeper*)
   e correct (also *imprisonment, incarceration*)
   f cage (also *cell*)
   g correct, though *autocrat* is not disapproving; *despot, tyrant* are

4 a in, in   f behind   k of
   b to, in   g under   l on
   c on   h through   m with
   d at   i on   n of
   e on   j in   o from, about

Grammar

5 a can pay
   b have to have / must have (also *need to have*)
   c could collect
   d may be borrowed
   e would have phoned, could
   f could/might have been injured
   g ought to have / should have reviewed
   h might have won
   i should have been / ought to have been
   j needn't have stayed / didn't have to stay
   k could/may be falling / have fallen
   l ought not to have agreed / shouldn't have agreed, would/might/could be
  m needed to have found / needed (to find) / had to find
   n could not have started
   o must have told
   p shouldn't drive
   q can't/couldn't have left

Use of English

6 1 ecstatic   6 graceful
   2 mournful   7 unearthly
   3 instinctive   8 (re)assurance
   4 spontaneous   9 anxieties
   5 assortment   10 improvisation

Unit 19
Reading
1 1 B 2 D 3 A 4 B 5 C 6 D 7 C

Vocabulary

2 The words are: apparition, ghost, ghoul, phantom, spectre, spirit, spook, wraith.
   a spirit   e spooked   i spectre
   b ghoulish   f spirited   j ghost
   c phantom   g apparitions k spirits
   d ghost   h wraith   l phantom

3 1 intelligent   6 panic   11 consciousness
   2 visions   7 rational   12 psyche
   3 mind   8 sense   13 unconscious
   4 pathologically 9 Primitive 14 images
   5 hallucinations 10 instincts

Grammar

4 *Suggested answers*
   a He sits alone in his room all day long / He sits all day long alone in his room, painstakingly writing up his findings by hand, mostly on scrap paper and usually in unfathomably long and complex sentences.
   b To my astonishment the fortune-teller's predictions turned out to be uncannily accurate.
   c Strangely enough, although it was practically dark, I was actually feeling quite relaxed as I waited patiently for a glimpse of the apparition, but naturally that changed dramatically when the room went cold all of a sudden.
   d I've never seen anything look quite so eerie or move so strangely – I was terrified out of my wits!
   e Curiously there hadn't been any further sightings of the ghost in the castle since the previous owner left last summer.
   f He was made up very realistically for the carnival the other day – he looked just like the ghost of an old woman.
   g He always speaks intelligently on the subject of the paranormal, but the talk he was giving later was generally expected to be even better than usual.
   h For some reason the computer in the back office started behaving rather oddly, inexplicably flashing up strangely disturbing messages onto the screen.
   i The light mysteriously came on suddenly, although no one was anywhere near the switch at the time.

Use of English

5 1 medium 2 figures 3 odd 4 mind 5 soul 6 fast

Unit 20
Use of English

1 1 the opposite
   2 it epitomises human fallibility which lies at the heart of comedy
   3 as deliberately cruel and vindictive
   4 comedy that includes a poetic dimension and/or acts as a vehicle for social criticism and/or goes into greater character depth and/or makes use of sentiment and realism

5 *Possible answer: 66 words*

The key elements of farce are clowning, slapstick and caricature, and, given their capacity to make people laugh out loud, they are present to some extent in the majority of comedies. Coming to the fore in the Middle Ages, farce also inspired the great comedy dramatists of the late 16th and 17th centuries, including Shakespeare, and still exists as a comic genre in its own right.

Grammar

2
a got; set up
b having/getting; cleaned
c had/got; stolen
d have; deliver (also *get; to deliver*)
e had; happen
f got/had; kitted out
g have; enjoying
h having/getting; analysed
i Have; wait (also *Get; to wait*)
j had/got; laughing
k have; throwing
l have; turned into
m get; to come (also *have; come*)
n had; fill out (also *got; to fill out*)
o have; arrested
p get; to meet
q got; caught
r got; finished
s get; telling
t got; working/to work (also *had; working*)
u had/had got; nesting

Vocabulary

3
a droll, facetious, humorous, hysterical, jocular
b beam, grin, smirk
c cackle, chuckle, giggle, roar, snigger, snort, titter
d beam, cackle, chuckle, giggle, grin, roar, smirk, snigger, snort, titter
e droll, facetious, humorous, hysterical, jocular
f cackle, chuckle, giggle, roar, snigger, snort, titter
g cackle (unpleasant to listen to), facetious (inappropriate), smirk (self-satisfied, disapproving), snigger (unkind), snort (can imply derision), titter (when something isn't intended to be funny)

4
a a go of
b go by
c to a stop
d stop off
e go into/over
f go up
g stop at
h stopped up
i gone down
j going in for
k a stop to
l a go at
m go off
n gone over
o stopping over/off

5 agree (*has* doesn't agree with *verbs*)
a end (*with* is a preposition)
b start (*And* is a conjunction)
c split (*to ever split* is a split infinitive)
d clichés (*like the plague* is a cliché)
e always (*always* is alliterative here)
f specific (*more or less* is not specific)
g unnecessary (this sentence includes two sets of parenthetical remarks)
h fragments (this is a sentence fragment)
i Contractions (this sentence includes two contractions)
j generalise (this is a generalisation)

k double (*don't use no* is a double negative)
l Avoid (the sentence contains both an ampersand and an abbreviation)
m commas (there are two unnecessary commas in this sentence)
n diminutive (*diminutive* is a big word)
o exclamation (the sentence ends with three exclamation marks)
p correctly (*irregardless* is incorrect)
q apostrophe (*it's* does not need an apostrophe, *its* does)
r Puns (*groan* is a pun on *grown*)
s Proofread (the word *left* has been omitted between *you* and *any*)

Use of English

6
1 so funny (that) his audiences end up in
2 she was upset, revenge was the last thing
3 daughter's wedding was concerned, nothing was too
4 you (can) turn a blind eye to
5 been on the go since she arrived
6 stopped short of telling her my real
7 had her car broken into by some youngsters
8 what I try, I can't get him to

Writing workout 1 **Letter**

1
1 clearly
2 strong
3 engage
4 Develop
5 balance
6 appropriate
7 Demonstrate
8 effectively
9 Use
10 logically
11 effective
12 grammar

2 1 c – opens clearly with a reason for writing (1), appropriate register (6), accurate grammar and spelling (12)
2 b – tries to engage the reader (3), develops the topic relevantly (4), appropriate register (6), uses a rhetorical question as an effective stylistic device (8), uses an example to reinforce a point (9), accurate grammar and spelling (12)
3 d – tries to engage the reader (3), develops the topic relevantly (4), appropriate register (6), demonstrates a wide range of vocabulary (7), uses an example to illustrate a point (9), accurate grammar and spelling (12)
4 a – ends on a strong note (2), appropriate register (6)

3 The only thing really wrong with the letter is the closing *Yours sincerely*, which should be *Yours faithfully* with the unnamed *Dear Sir*. Otherwise the letter reflects the advice in exercise 1 well.

4 The order is **b, a, d, c, e.**

Optional writing task
If possible, show your letter to your teacher. Otherwise, once you have worked through exercises 5–8, compare it with the version in the Key for exercise 8.

5 I tend to think of play as spontaneous behaviour that has no clear-cut goal and does not conform to a stereotypical pattern and your article would seem to encourage this view. To me the purpose of play is simply play itself; it appears to be pleasurable. But play also has benefits: it is key to an individual's development, social relationships and status.

6
1 As
2 not only
3 but also
4 Furthermore
5 while
6 as
7 In my view
8 namely

7 *Recent* research *suggests* that play may be as important to life for us and other *animals* as sleeping and dreaming. And no-one would *dispute* that play is an important part of a *healthy*, happy childhood. But if play is necessary for the *physical* and *social* development of young animals, *including* humans, what *happens* if young creatures are *prevented* from playing or *maltreated* with the result that their play is *abnormal*? Their *development* may also be abnormal. *Certainly* the *behaviour* of 'problem dogs' *invariably* develops through *improper* games or lack of games when they were young.

8 **5 a   6 d   7 c**
Dear Sir
Your delightful article on play behaviour among animals is a poignant reminder of just how fascinating wildlife can be. However, it also throws into sharp relief some interesting and far-reaching questions on the purpose of play, which the writer failed to discuss. Adults and young, alone and together, mammals and many birds play – but why? Do they gain anything from these exuberant displays, or do they do it just because it feels good? I tend to think of play as spontaneous behaviour that has no clear-cut goal and does not conform to a stereotypical pattern and your article would seem to encourage this view. To me the purpose of play is simply play itself; it appears to be pleasurable. But play also has benefits: it is key to an individual's development, social relationships and status.

As a dog-owner, I know play is vital for proper development in dogs: games of keep away, chase and tug-of-war not only develop physical abilities but also help the animals attain social status by establishing superior mental and physical skills. Furthermore, play, while it often mimics aggression, as in the article, is one form of defence used to defuse potential confrontations. In my view, ritualised play in humans, namely sports, serves an identical purpose.

Recent research suggests that play may be as important to life for us and other animals as sleeping and dreaming. And no-one would dispute that play is an important part of a healthy, happy childhood. But if play is necessary for the physical and social development of young animals, including humans, what happens if young creatures are prevented from playing or maltreated with the result that their play is abnormal? Their development may also be abnormal. Certainly the behaviour of 'problem dogs' invariably develops through improper games or lack of games when they were young.

Today millions of children spend endless hours watching television and playing computer games instead of playing with one another. How are they going to learn to deal with a world that is becoming more complicated all the time, I wonder? As successfully as Hudson?
Yours faithfully
(352 words)

Writing workout 2 Review

1 a, c, d, e, f, g, h, i. A review should only include a brief summary of what is being reviewed, not full details (b), and personal anecdotes and hearsay (j) are also inappropriate.

2 Neither text is a complete review, but Text B is compiled from authentic review material. This is clear from its reference to a specific playwright/play/production, the brief descriptive synopsis and the evaluative comments / expressed opinions. Text A is from a biographical entry on Pinter in *The Oxford Companion to English Literature*.

Optional writing task
If possible, show your review to your teacher. Otherwise, once you have worked through exercises 3–9, compare it with the version in the Key for 9.

3 1 allusions
2 dense
3 character
4 mysterious
5 like chasing a drop of water through a fountain
6 directed
7 playwright
8 metaphysical
9 immediate
10 packed

4 On the page, Harold Pinter's *No Man's Land* is enough to give the reader a panic attack. The literary allusions are so dense, the dislocation of character so mysterious that pinning down what's going on is like chasing a drop of water through a fountain. But it's striking how little this matters in performance. Directed by the playwright at London's Lyttleton Theatre, this most metaphysical of Pinter's plays is immediate, fully fleshed, packed with social detail. It is also very funny.

5 **1 b   2 h   3 d   4 a   5 g   6 e**
7 i   8 k   9 j   10 f   11 c   12 l
The two *central characters* are *seeming opposites*. They are bound together by a *hidden affinity*. Hirst is a successful *literary man*. He lives in an *imposing house* in Hampstead. Hirst invites Spooner home. Spooner is a seedy pub worker from Chalk Farm. The spaciousness of Hirst's life, and the achievements, represent everything that Spooner has dreamed of. For Hirst, Spooner is what he might have become. We are not dealing with a *simple contrast* between success and failure. Hirst's success has turned to ashes. He is a *heavy drinker*, essentially isolated (apart from the presence of two dubious servants), living in a state of *moral paralysis*. Spooner only outwardly embodies what he has escaped. The *shabby guest* is an emanation of the well-dressed host's *inner emptiness*. There is a sense of *tragic waste* in the play, of things left undone and of unappeased ghosts. There is some fine comedy. The new production does *equal justice* to both aspects.

6 The two central characters are seeming opposites who are bound together by a hidden affinity. Hirst is a successful literary man living in an imposing house in Hampstead. Spooner, whom Hirst invites home, is a seedy pub worker from Chalk Farm. The spaciousness of Hirst's life, and the achievements, represent everything that Spooner has dreamed of. For Hirst, on the other hand, Spooner is what he might have become if things had gone wrong for him. Not that we are dealing with a simple contrast between success and failure. Hirst's success has turned to ashes. He is a heavy drinker, essentially isolated (apart from the presence of two dubious servants), living in a state of moral paralysis. It is only outwardly that Spooner embodies what he has escaped. The shabby guest is also an emanation of the well-dressed host's inner emptiness. There is a sense of tragic waste in the play, of things left undone and of unappeased ghosts. At the same time, it is the occasion for some fine comedy and the new production does equal justice to both aspects.

7 *Suggested answers*
1 g **2** f **3** b **4** i **5** d **6** a **7** c **8** h **9** e

8 *Suggested answer*
I must confess I find the temperature of the play drops somewhat when the two manservants appear. To me they are figures out of the Pinter repertory, whereas Hirst and Spooner spring straight from his imagination, but they make their contribution to a powerful and satisfying evening.

9 *Possible answer: 362 words*
On the page, Harold Pinter's *No Man's Land* is enough to give the reader a panic attack. The literary allusions are so dense, the dislocation of character so mysterious that pinning down what's going on is like chasing a drop of water through a fountain. But it's striking how little this matters in performance. Directed by the playwright at London's Lyttleton Theatre, this most metaphysical of Pinter's plays is immediate, fully fleshed, packed with social detail. It is also very funny.

The two central characters are seeming opposites who are bound together by a hidden affinity. Hirst is a successful literary man living in an imposing house in Hampstead. Spooner, whom Hirst invites home, is a seedy pub worker from Chalk Farm. The spaciousness of Hirst's life, and the achievements, represent everything that Spooner has dreamed of. For Hirst, on the other hand, Spooner is what he might have become if things had gone wrong for him.

Not that we are dealing with a simple contrast between success and failure. Hirst's success has turned to ashes. He is a heavy drinker, essentially isolated (apart from the presence of two dubious servants), living in a state of moral paralysis. It is only outwardly that Spooner embodies what he has escaped. The shabby guest is also an emanation of the well-dressed host's inner emptiness. There is a sense of tragic waste in the play, of things left undone and of unappeased ghosts. At the same time, it is the occasion for some fine comedy and the new production does equal justice to both aspects.

The leads are terrific. Corin Redgrave as Hirst and John Wood as Spooner both give superlative performances. Wood is entertainingly shambling and unsettlingly cunning, while Redgrave oscillates between frosty superciliousness and bleary-eyed flailing. Though Danny Dyer is flat as one manservant, Andy de la Tour is both threatening and ingratiating as the other.

I must confess I find the temperature of the play drops somewhat when the two manservants appear. To me they are figures out of the Pinter repertory, whereas Hirst and Spooner spring straight from his imagination, but they make their contribution to a powerful and satisfying evening.

Writing Workout 3 **Essay**

1 **1** b **2** a **3** b **4** a **5** b

2 Any of the points could be included. Whether or not they were, and how they would be ordered, would depend on the argument presented.

Optional writing task
If possible, show your essay to your teacher. Otherwise, once you have worked through exercises 3–6, compare it with the version in the Key for 6.

3 The essay includes points: b, c, e, g, h, i, j, k, n, o, p, q, r, s, t.

4 Early unmanned rockets gave way first to manned orbital missions, then to moon landings and more recently to a manned space station, while probe-mounted cameras now *speed their way* round the solar system, bringing more and more spectacular images of more and more distant planets directly into our living rooms.

These achievements speak for themselves and none of them would have been possible without the *significant investments* of time and money that have been made by the nations *at the forefront of developments*. There can, therefore, be no question that space exploration has been an investment in the future – or that it still is, the prospect of permanent space stations *yet to be fulfilled*, let alone the more futuristic notion of full-blown space colonies *accommodating fugitives* from an overpopulated or *environmentally devastated* world.

Surely the real question, however, is not whether space exploration *represents* an investment in the future but whether the investment it represents *constitutes* a *worthwhile* one in terms of *return*. *There is a school of thought that sees space exploration as indispensable* both for *increasing our understanding of* the universe, earth and our origins, and for its unforeseeable practical results in terms of technology and resources. Indeed the practical applications of technological know-how that is *acquired* in the first instance through space research *are regularly cited* as examples of *the wider benefits of* space exploration and *certainly it is true* that, thanks to the space programmes, television pictures can now *be transmitted* live around the world and non-stick frying pans can be used in the kitchen. But *how has that relieved the suffering of* the earth's starving millions?

Poverty, hunger, disease and war are *the world's greatest enemies* and if the nations that dominate the space scene devoted half as much money and effort to these problems as they do to space exploration much could be done to *alleviate* them. For the first time in history, the technological resources to combat human suffering really do exist, yet they are syphoned off for investment in a future that, for many, will never come.

5 Sentence **a** is too short and informal to make a good opening sentence for an essay. Also the link with the question in the title of the essay is not immediately obvious.
Sentence **b** links both to the title and to the discussion of the topic that follows. It is clear and the language and register are both appropriate.
Sentence **c** merely reiterates the question in the essay title without introducing the essay or in any way pointing forward to what is to come.

6 *Possible final version: 339 words*
Space exploration has come a long way since its first tentative beginnings. Early unmanned rockets gave way first to manned orbital missions, then to moon landings and more recently to a manned space station, while probe-mounted cameras now speed their way round the solar system, bringing ~~more and more~~ spectacular images of ~~more and more~~ distant planets directly into our living rooms.

These achievements speak for themselves and none of them would have been possible without ~~the~~ significant investments of time and money ~~that have been made by the nations at the forefront of developments~~. There can, therefore, be no question that space exploration has been an investment in the future – or that it still is, the prospect of permanent space stations yet to be fulfilled~~, let alone the more futuristic notion of full-blown space colonies accommodating fugitives from an overpopulated or environmentally devastated world~~.

Surely the real question, however, is not whether space exploration represents an investment in the future but whether the investment it represents constitutes a worthwhile one in terms of return. ~~There is a school of thought that sees space exploration as indispensable both for increasing~~ *There is no doubt that space exploration has increased* our understanding of the universe, earth and our origins, and ~~for its~~ *yielded* unforeseeable practical results in terms of technology and resources. Indeed the practical applications of technological know-how that ~~is~~ *has been* acquired through space research ~~in the first instance~~ are regularly cited as examples of the wider benefits of space exploration and certainly it is true ~~that, thanks to the space programmes, television pictures can now be transmitted live around the world and non-stick frying pans can be used in the kitchen~~ *that space programmes are to thank for the possibility of live global television pictures and non-stick frying pans.* But how has that relieved the suffering of the earth's starving millions?

Poverty, hunger, disease and war are the world's greatest enemies and if the nations that dominate the space scene devoted half as much money and effort to these problems as they do to space exploration much could be done to alleviate them. For the first time in history, the technological resources to combat human suffering really do exist, yet they are syphoned off for investment in a future that, for many, will never come.

In that context, surely space exploration is a luxury we can ill afford. Isn't it time to invest our time and energy in putting our earthly house in order and let space look after itself until we have?

Writing workout 4 **Proposal**

1
1	document	5	recommendations	9	convictions
2	evaluated	6	convince	10	succinct
3	justifies	7	language	11	formal/ neutral
4	forward-looking	8	points	12	punchy

2 1 d 2 f 3 a 4 c 5 e 6 b

Optional writing task
If possible, show your proposal to your teacher. Otherwise, once you have worked through exercises 3–9, compare it with the version in the Key for exercise 9.

3 **Options:** a, d, j, n
Benefits: c, e, f, h, i, k, m, o
Background: b, g, l

4 1 Benefits + C
Understanding the role the spiritual dimension can play in our lives helps build *better relationships at work* and thus enables people to *work more effectively* . [Furthermore,] a spiritually-friendly workplace is [more than just] a *nice place to work.* It can also be *more profitable*, with *greater staff retention rates*, hence lower recruitment costs, and it can see an *increase in creativity and innovation, improved morale and teamwork*, and *an improvement of the interface between the organisation and its customer-base.*

2 Options + A
Yoga, t'ai chi, poetry seminars and *workshops on philosophy, theatre or painting* can all help to ease stress and get a better balance between work and home.

3 Background + B
Organisational psychologists specialising in *the link between work and well-being* [cannot] highlight [strongly enough] *the importance of appealing to employees' hearts and souls* as well as their minds and pockets: *people need to be able to make a life, not just a living.*

5 1 clear – beyond dispute; can – stand to
2 over-expensive – cost-prohibitive
3 common – widespread; looking – searching
A help – serve; ease – alleviate; get – promote; better – healthier
B highlight – stress
C part – role; side – dimension

6 They could all be omitted, but the writing would lose impact and be less persuasive as a result.

7 Experts predict that understanding the spiritual will become *such an important* part of workplace human development *that* it will *begin to regularly* feature in management training and will *eventually* have a place *in some form or another* in every organisation, *no matter how small.*

8 Introducing spirituality to this workplace now would ~~make everyone happy~~ *not only be unanimously welcomed,* ~~be good now~~ *it would also reap immediate benefits* for all involved ~~and~~ *as well as* ~~be good over time~~ *offer long-term rewards* ~~with~~ *in the guise of* a more productive workforce and increased profitability. At the same time, ~~the possible effect~~ *the potential impact* on the organisation's internal and external relations ~~would be big~~ *should not be underestimated;* ~~so would the use~~ *neither should the PR value to the organisation* of being ~~involved in such developments~~ *at the forefront of the workplace spiritual revolution.*

9 *Suggested answer: 373 words including subheadings*
Introduction
The purpose of this proposal is to advocate the introduction of an element of spirituality in the workplace, this now being widely recognised as one of the most effective means of enhancing the working environment for the future.
Background
With 24-hour work-orientated culture the norm and stress at work widespread, growing numbers of people are searching for deeper meaning to life. Organisational psychologists specialising in the link between work and well-being cannot stress strongly enough the importance of appealing to employees' hearts and souls as well as their minds and pockets: people need to be able to make a life, not just a living.
Options
Spirituality in the workplace can take many forms. None are difficult to introduce and, above all, none are cost-prohibitive. Yoga, t'ai chi, poetry seminars and workshops on philosophy, theatre or painting can all serve to alleviate stress and promote a healthier balance between work and home.
Benefits
The value to employees of such measures is beyond dispute, but research shows that employers too stand to gain enormously. Understanding the role the spiritual dimension can play in our lives helps build better relationships at work and thus enables people to work more effectively. Furthermore, a spiritually-friendly workplace is more than just a nice place to work. It can also be more profitable, with greater staff retention rates, hence lower recruitment costs, and it can see an increase in creativity and innovation, improved morale and teamwork, and an improvement of the interface between the organisation and its customer-base.
Looking ahead
Experts predict that understanding the spiritual will become such an important part of workplace human development that it will begin to regularly feature in management training and will eventually have a place in some form or another in every organisation, no matter how small.

Conclusion

Introducing spirituality to this workplace now would not only be unanimously welcomed, it would also reap immediate benefits for all involved as well as offer long-term rewards in the guise of a more productive workforce and increased profitability. At the same time, the potential impact on the organisation's internal and external relations should not be underestimated; neither should the PR value to the organisation of being at the forefront of the workplace spiritual revolution.

Writing workout 5 **Article**

1 1 B   3 H   5 A   7 A   9 H
   2 B   4 H   6 B   8 H   10 H

2 1 A adventure B commuting   4 B economy A performance
   2 B convenience A power   5 B practicality A thrills
   3 A glamour B reliability   6 B comfort A style

3 1 aerodynamic   5 control
   2 handling   6 cruiser
   3 spacious   7 commuter
   4 motorcycle   8 machines

Optional writing task
If possible, show your article to your teacher. Otherwise, once you have worked through exercises 4–9, compare it with the version in the Key for exercise 9.

4 **a** There is a clear angle here which relates well to the magazine feature topic. The paragraph is well constructed and quite informative, though likely to appeal more to existing riders than possible newcomers. The style and tone are neutral and appropriate for most purposes, though the paragraph is a bit bland.

   b This paragraph aims to involve and intrigue the reader from the outset, using a personal approach. Again there is a clear angle which relates well to the magazine feature topic and again the paragraph is quite informative. This time, though, potential new riders may well be intrigued to read on. The style and tone are direct and informal with good use of stylistic devices – well-suited to a college magazine.

   c This paragraph doesn't have a clear angle that relates to the magazine feature topic, neither does it sit well as an article opener – apparently quite complete in itself for what it is. The approach is too personal and the style rather colloquial.

5 1 just   3 still   5 To date   7 All
   2 already 4 but   6 along with 8 when
The paragraph is closest in style to b in exercise 4.

6 **a** trips   **e** ground
   b road   **f** 120 kph
   c transportation **g** stops
   d running   **h** machine

7 And the source of such a wonderful mix of convenience, economy and adventure? Well, it's a Honda, but not a Fireblade – a Foresight. Yes, 250cc of value for money and dependability, packaged in *stylish, windcheating bodywork*, with a *large, comfortable seat* and a *secure luggage compartment*. It won't pull wheelies, but it will hold a steady 120 kph and comfortably cover 700+ kilometres without refuelling.

8 All four boxes could apply. *Possible answer*
Together we've criss-crossed Europe from east to west and north to south, we've made our way through the heat and dust of the Middle East's deserts and we've negotiated some of Africa's most spectacular bush roads. That's a lot to ask of a 4x4, let alone a two-wheeler, but not only has the Foresight lived up to all my hopes in terms of its long distance capability, it's also inspired confidence along the way and stood up well to some pretty arduous conditions. Apart from a few little dents and scratches (adventure scars!), it still looks like new. So, motorcycle or scooter? As far as I'm concerned, there's only one answer to that question. The only other question is where to go next …

9 **a** This is the catchiest of the three titles and points forward to the article in a way **b** and **c** don't. It also avoids the (potentially alienating) use of the first person I.

Full version: 323 words including title
Travelling with Foresight …
Mention motorbikes and most people think of speed, excitement, glamour, adventure and the freedom of the open road. Mention scooters, on the other hand, and more mundane considerations like economy, comfort, convenience, practicality and reliability probably come to mind. Yet scooters are currently the fastest growing sector of the two-wheeled market. Are they really all bought by sad individuals who can't hack a real bike? If that's what you think, read on and prepare to be surprised.

At just over 15 months old, the two-wheeler I own has clocked up 50,000 km already and is still going strong. It was purchased for travel, not for showing off or racing between motorway service areas, but for covering long distances economically, conveniently and comfortably. To date, we have covered 34 different countries on various adventure expeditions, along with the more usual convenient commuting at home – all on incredibly low fuel consumption, sustaining motorway speeds when not off the beaten track.

And the source of such a wonderful mix of convenience, economy and adventure? Well, it's a Honda, but not a Fireblade – a Foresight. Yes, 250cc of value for money and dependability, packaged in stylish, windcheating bodywork, with a large, comfortable seat and a secure luggage compartment. It won't pull wheelies, but it will hold a steady 120 kph and comfortably cover 700+ kilometres without refuelling.

Together we've criss-crossed Europe from east to west and north to south, we've made our way through the heat and dust of the Middle East's deserts and we've negotiated some of Africa's most spectacular bush roads. That's a lot to ask of a 4x4, let alone a two-wheeler, but not only has the Foresight lived up to all my hopes in terms of its long distance capability, it's also inspired confidence along the way and stood up well to some pretty arduous conditions. Apart from a few little dents and scratches (adventure scars!), it still looks like new. So, motorcycle or scooter? As far as I'm concerned, there's only one answer to that question. The only other question is where to go next …

Writing workout 6 Report

1 1 e 2 a 3 f 4 h 5 i 6 d 7 b 8 c 9 g

2 The course is for people who need to design and produce printed material on a computer without having had any relevant training. DTP is *desktop publishing*.

Optional writing task
If possible, show your report to your teacher. Otherwise, once you have worked through exercises 3–7, compare it with the version in the Key for exercise 7.

3 The paragraph starts more like a letter (*My reason for writing ...*), the purpose of the report is unclear and personal references (*My/I/me*) are best avoided in reports. Although it can be a good idea to summarise a report's content in the introduction, this should be brief. Here *Let me begin ...* is inappropriate style for a report and the final sentence (*I'll then ... recommendation.*) sounds more like an oral presentation than a written report.

Possible rewrite:
The purpose of this report is to review and assess *Good Design using DTP* with a view to determining its suitability as a course for other untrained DTP users within this organisation. The report looks first at general arrangements, before going on to course content and concluding with an evaluation.

4 *Possible answer: 114 words*
The course took place at The Training Centre in Regent Street, London, on January 13–14. The facilities and back-up at the centre were excellent. The computing room was a good size, well equipped and comfortable; each participant had a dedicated computer terminal for the course duration.

The course was attended by a total of seven participants, all of whom had had some experience of – but no training in – DTP. Essentially it was a homogeneous group of beginners with compatible interests and abilities.

Arrangements throughout were faultless and timings consistently punctual. There was a good supply of refreshments during the day and considerable trouble had been taken with the lunches, which were very enjoyable.

5 *Corrected paragraph: 72 words*
The *two*-day programme was quite intensive, covering a range of DTP functions and features, including:
- what *soft*ware to use
- typography and fonts
- layout and balance
- graphics and logos
- colour considerations
- proofing and printing

Throughout the course was highly *practical*, with ample exercises and opportunities for hands-on practice. Comprehensive notes were provided for reference and participants were also given a copy of their completed work on disk.

6 The style and tone are too informal for a report. Colloquial expressions like *chap*, *knows a thing or two*, etc., are inappropriate, as are the contracted verb forms, the repeated use of personal pronouns, the direct question and the use of the imperative.

Possible rewrite:
The tutor was Cambridge-based Will Render, a well-known expert who teaches regularly at the centre. He is obviously very knowledgeable about DTP and he is also a skilled teacher. His approach was extremely accommodating, seeking to tailor aspects of the course to suit group and individual requirements as far as possible.

The course was both enjoyable and informative, equipping participants with a sound grasp of the mechanics of DTP but also, perhaps more importantly, engendering the interest and confidence to use DTP to full effect within their professional lives. In my opinion, anyone using DTP without a design background would benefit enormously from this course.

7 *Possible answer: 352 words*
Good Design using DTP
The purpose of this report is to review and assess *Good Design using DTP* with a view to determining its suitability as a course for other untrained DTP users within this organisation. The report looks first at general arrangements, before going on to course content and concluding with an evaluation.

General arrangements
The course took place at The Training Centre in Regent Street, London, on January 13–14. The facilities and back-up at the centre were excellent. The computing room was a good size, well equipped and comfortable; each participant had a dedicated computer terminal for the course duration.

The course was attended by a total of seven participants, all of whom had had some experience of – but no training in – DTP. Essentially it was a homogeneous group of beginners with compatible interests and abilities.

Arrangements throughout were faultless and timings consistently punctual. There was a good supply of refreshments during the day and considerable trouble had been taken with the lunches, which were very enjoyable.

Course content
The two-day programme was quite intensive, covering a range of DTP functions and features, including:
- what software to use
- typography and fonts
- layout and balance
- graphics and logos
- colour considerations
- proofing and printing

Throughout the course was highly practical, with ample exercises and opportunities for hands-on practice. Comprehensive notes were provided for reference and participants were also given a copy of their completed work on disk.

The tutor was Cambridge-based Will Render, a well-known expert who teaches regularly at the centre. He is obviously very knowledgeable about DTP and he is also a skilled teacher. His approach was extremely accommodating, seeking to tailor aspects of the course to suit group and individual requirements as far as possible.

Evaluation and recommendation
The course was both enjoyable and informative, equipping participants with a sound grasp of the mechanics of DTP but also, perhaps more importantly, engendering the interest and confidence to use DTP to full effect within their professional lives. In my opinion, anyone using DTP without a design background would benefit enormously from this course.

HWLC LEARNING CENTRE